Compact Guide: Bermuda is the ideal quick-reference guide to this group of tiny islands located off the East Coast of the USA but maintaining very British traditions. It tells you everything you need to know about their attractions, from the beguiling architecture and the culture of Hamilton to breathtaking beaches and diving among colourful coral reefs and ancient shipwrecks.

This is one of more than 100 titles in Insight Guides' series of pocket-sized, easy-to-use guidebooks edited for the independent-minded traveller. Compact Guides are in essence travel encyclopedias in miniature, designed to be comprehensive yet portable, as well as up-to-date and authoritative.

Peters
743-4999

Star Attractions

An instant reference to some of Bermuda's top attractions to help you set your priorities.

Gombey dancers p18

The birdcage p19

Johnny Barnes p30

Golf p33

Somerset Bridge p35

Long Bay p38

Bermuda Aquarium, Museum & Zoo p50

Crystal Cave p54

The Railway Trail p68

Sir George Somers p73

Moon gate p72

BeRMUDa

Introduction

Places

Culture

Leisure

Practical Information

Bermuda – Atlantic Paradise

Opposite: bright colours in St George

A beautiful island in the Atlantic Ocean basking in the sun, fringed with pale pink beaches washed by turquoise waters. Friendly people, and captivating architecture. Summer almost the year-round. More golf courses per square mile than any place else on earth. Fishing boats bobbing in lovely harbours. Superb snorkelling and scuba diving, and some of the world's greatest fishing. A place to kick back and relax, or play as much tennis and squash as you like, or explore ancient forts and caves and sophisticated art galleries.

Hamilton Harbour

If you think it sounds like paradise, you're not alone. After a harrowing ocean voyage in the 19th century, the American writer and humorist Mark Twain, a frequent island visitor, famously remarked, 'Bermuda is paradise, but you have to go through hell to get to it.'

Bermuda does have a little something for everyone – except for mountain-climbers, or snowbunnies. And those in search of glitzy casinos, neon-decorated discos, drive-through volcanoes, and funky little bazaars where you hunker down and bargain for your goods will search in vain.

Colonial traditions remain

5

It's almost as if a chunk of Great Britain broke away in the distant past and drifted across the Atlantic Ocean, settling in a sun-kissed spot off the coast of the United States. Tea is served each day at four o'clock, and centuries-old ceremonies are performed by bagpipers wearing kilts. In June, Bermudians celebrate the Queen's birthday with pomp and circumstance, and cricket and rugby are played with great enthusiasm.

Bermuda has something of a storybook quality about it. Its limestone houses and buildings are small and sherbet-coloured,with snow-white sloping rooftops glistening in the sunshine. They enhance a landscape that is awash with semitropical greenery and flowers. Even the cars are small, tootling around narrow winding roads.

The island is as clean as a whistle. Streets are edged with hibiscus, croton, oleander, and morning glories, and tall royal palms reach for the sky. The air is crystal-clear, and so pollution-free that rainwater cascades off rooftops and falls into cisterns, ready to drink. Since there are no freshwater lakes in Bermuda, the island has to rely on rainwater for drinking.

Geography

Christopher Columbus, who famously sailed the ocean blue in fourteen hundred and ninety-two, did not land on Bermuda. These islands lie north of the route that took him across the Atlantic and through the Caribbean Sea. But Columbus did pave the

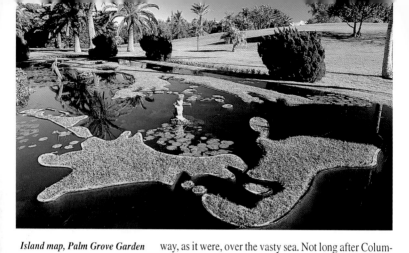

Island map, Palm Grove Garden

Royal Naval Dockyard

way, as it were, over the vasty sea. Not long after Columbus's first voyage – around 1503 – the islands were first sighted, by the Spanish explorer Juan de Bermudez.

Shaped like a fish-hook, Bermuda lies 1,046 km (650 miles) east of Cape Hatteras, North Carolina, 1,246 km (774 miles) from New York, and 4,828 km (3,000 miles) from London. It is only 57 sq km (22 sq miles) – 34 km (21 miles) long and not even 3 km (2 miles) wide at its broadest point. You can see the deep blue ocean from almost any place on the island, which means that you're never far from one of those pink sandy beaches.

The largest town on the island – Hamilton, the capital – has fewer than 2,000 residents. Hamilton is roughly in the centre of the island, and sits on a beautiful harbour. The town of St George's in the east end is quite small, and Somerset village in the west end is scarcely more than a wide place in the road.

Many people think Bermuda is somewhere in the Caribbean, while others assume it's in the Bahamas. It is neither. It's smack out in the Atlantic Ocean. From the island's earliest beginnings, Bermudians have been seafarers and shipbuilders; they had little choice, given their remoteness. Needless to say, sailing and yachting are among the more actively pursued endeavours in these waters. The yacht race held every year in June from Newport, Rhode Island, to Bermuda is a huge event, and Bermudians love the annual Non-Mariners' Race, when landlubbers tie and glue together all sorts of clumsy crafts and race them at Mangrove Bay.

Bermuda is actually not one island of volcanic origin: it is a collection of more than 150 islands, small and large, many of them uninhabited. If you consider even the tiniest, there are more than 350 islands. But the many bridges that string the seven largest of the islands together are constructed in such a way that there is very little sense of island-hopping – which is, in actual fact, what you're doing when you scoot around the 'island.'

In 1612, three years after the accidental discovery of Bermuda, by means of the shipwreck of the *Sea Venture*, England sent settlers to these islands, and the Somers Island Company was founded to manage the new colony. In 1616, Sir Richard Norwood made the first survey of the island, and Bermuda was divided into 'tribes', which are now called parishes. Each parish bears the name of one of the investors in the 17th-century company: Pembroke, Hamilton, Devonshire, Smith's, Warwick, Paget, Southampton, and Sandys. St George's Island, named in part for Admiral Sir George Somers and in part for the patron saint of England, was a public common in the early 17th century. The Tribe Roads that cross the island from North to South date from that first survey.

It's almost impossible to get lost in Bermuda, at least not while travelling east to west. There are four main east-west routes: North Shore Road, Middle Road, Harbour Road, and South Road. There are scores of north-south roads that wind and twist, and here it is possible to lose your way. But it is never difficult to figure out where you are, and friendly Bermudians will happily set you straight.

Ride on South Shore

Climate

Bermuda is a semi-tropical island with essentially two seasons: spring and summer. During the summer (roughly mid-May till mid-November, with the warmest months July, August, and early September), temperatures may not rise above 32°C (89°F), but it can feel much warmer because of the extremely high humidity. Summer evening temperatures are about 5°C (10°F) cooler.

Mid-November through April, the thermometer hovers in the low 20s Centigrade (low 70s Fahrenheit) down to the mid-teens Centigrade (60s Fahrenheit), but, again, high humidity can chill the bones. The coolest months are January, February, and early March. The hurricane season runs from 1 June till the end of November, and while the island can be buffeted by high winds and heavy rains, it is rarely hit with full hurricane force.

Bermuda shorts and wide-brimmed hats are de rigueur

Population and economy

Little more than 58,000 people call Bermuda home. Sixty-one percent of the population is black, 39 percent is white. An amazing 64 percent of the islanders have a heritage of several generations here. Sixteen percent of the people are of English descent; 11 percent West Indian, and 9 percent Portuguese.

It may have been that a Portuguese ship was wrecked on Bermuda in 1543, and sailors from the ship made crude markings of what appear to be letters and a cross on what

is called Spanish Rock in the Spittal Pond Nature Reserve. (Spanish Rock itself no longer exists, but a plaster of Paris model is displayed in the Bermuda Historical Society Museum in Hamilton, and a bronze plaque in Spittal Pond marks where the rock was found by the early settlers.) The markings were quite rough, but historians believe that the carved letters 'RP' may have represented *Rex Portugaline* (King of Portugal), and that the cross represented the Portuguese Order of Christ. If that is true, then the Portuguese were among the first to set foot on these islands, but it was not until the mid-19th century that emigrants from Portugal began to move across the ocean, to the Atlantic Coast of the United States, to the West Indies, and to Bermuda.

Spittal Pond Nature Reserve

In 1847, the Bermuda government enacted legislation that permitted bounties to be paid to pirate ships that brought Portuguese settlers to these shores, and in the early 20th century the government imported people from the Azores, principally to work in the burgeoning tourist trade. Bermudians of Portuguese ancestry are descendants of those importations.

Slavery began early in Bermuda's history. The first Indian and the first black people (who may or may not have been slaves) were brought to the island in 1616, four years after the colony was established. For the most part, the black people who were brought as slaves came not from Africa but from the West Indies or the Americas. In 1619, a large importation of slaves, probably brought in on a pirate ship, were presented as a gift to Governor Miles Kimball. Not all the slaves were black: in the 17th century, white slaves were brought to Bermuda after Oliver Cromwell's victory, and there were also Indian slaves. About 30 Indian women were imported as slaves in 1644. By 1670, the government was attempting to curtail if not the institution of slavery at least the further importation of slaves to so small an island.

A shipping and sailing nation

From its beginnings, Bermuda has been a shipping and sailing nation, and slavery here was very different from that which existed in the United States and the Caribbean. There have never been vast sugar plantations, or huge tracts of land to be worked. Some slaves worked in the merchant fleet, but most were either household servants or trained as carpenters or masons.

There were at least three rebellions in the 17th century, and not all were initiated by slaves. Apparently there were at the time also free black people on the island. It is recorded that in 1656, a proclamation was issued by which all free blacks were banished from Bermuda and sent to Eleutheria in the Bahamas. While there were isolated incidents over a 200-year period, and some of them ugly, Bermuda never saw a mass slave uprising or a civil war over slavery. The institution of slavery was abolished on the island for good in 1834.

Bermuda has the second highest standard of living in the world, second only to the United States. There is no income tax, no sales tax, and virtually no unemployment. The average income is around $35,000 a year. The crime rate is very low. There are no slums. Despite being a British colony, Bermuda's economy is tied to the US. The Bermudian dollar is pegged to the US dollar, and Bermudian and US currency are used interchangeably.

Bermuda flowers at the Arboretum

Bermuda's earliest history is closely tied to that of the young United States. In 1609, the new British Colony of Jamestown, Virginia, was in dire straits, suffering from starvation. In England, the Virginia Company, which administered the colony, sent a fleet of ships carrying supplies and more colonists to Jamestown. The flagship of the fleet, the *Sea Venture*, was captained by Christopher Newport, who had led the first expedition to Jamestown, and on board was Thomas Gates, deputy governor of Jamestown. The fleet was under the command of Admiral Sir George Somers, who was also aboard the flagship. In a fierce storm, the *Sea Venture* was separated from the other ships, and wrecked off the northeast coast of Bermuda. The shipwreck was the catalyst for the colonisation of Bermuda, and many historians believe it was also the basis for Shakespeare's play, *The Tempest,* which is why you'll see so many sights in Bermuda with names from the play, such as Prospero, Caliban, and Ariel.

9

Politics and government

Great Britain's oldest colony, Bermuda has the world's second oldest Parliament, after England. In 1620, upon instructions by the Somers Island Company, the first Parliament met in St Peter's Church in St George's, under Governor Nathaniel Butler. Bermuda is a self-governing British crown colony, and remains so after a 1996 referendum on independence was defeated.

Bermuda's present form of government and its present constitution were adopted during elections held in 1968. The bicameral Parliament is comprised of the House of Assembly and the Senate. While the head of state is the British monarch and the Governor of Bermuda is appointed by the Queen, the Premier and the 40 members of the House of Assembly are elected by Bermudians. The Premier appoints 12 cabinet members, as well as five members of the 11-member Senate. Of the other six members of the Senate, three are selected by the Governor and three by the opposition leader. Members of both houses of Parliament sit for five-year terms. Bermuda's two primary political parties are the conservative United Bermuda Party, which has long been in power, and the left-

Colonial remnants: flag and Bank of Bermuda crest

Dishing out justice

leaning Progressive Labour Party. The current Governor is Thorold Masefield, and the Premier, leader of the United Bermuda Party, is Pamela Gordon – the first woman to hold that office in Bermuda, elected in 1997.

Tourism

Queen Victoria's daughter, Louise, came to the island in 1883, and her visit is credited with kicking off Bermuda's tourism industry. (The Hamilton Princess Hotel, built the following year, was named in her honour.) Tourism today is the number one industry on the island, but international banking is also a major concern. Other significant businesses include oil, insurance, computer software, shipping, and communications. More than 8,000 offshore companies are based on the island.

Each year well over a half million people visit Bermuda. Most come by air, but during the summer high season sleek cruise ships dock in Hamilton, St George's, and Royal Naval Dockyard. The majority of Bermuda's visitors come from the United States and Canada. Such a preponderance of Americans come from the East Coast that Bermuda doesn't promote the island in other parts of the US.

Tourists come in search of the usual island treasures – sun, sea, and sand. And golf. And they find all of that in great abundance. But this island is also a shopper's paradise. The shops of Hamilton, St George's, and Dockyard, are chock-full of cashmere, woollens, leather, china, crystal, wristwatches, electronic goods, upmarket perfumes and cosmetics, all sold at substantial discounts.

Visitors' primary complaint about Bermuda is that it is so expensive. It is expensive, but that is because absolutely everything is imported. There are small farms, but almost no manufacturing is done on the island, so everything from candy bars to cars comes from elsewhere.

Dockyard buoys

Bermuda is not an ideal vacation spot for children. Kids enjoy the Aquarium and some of the watersports, but there is precious little else for the little ones. Only a handful of the resort hotels have childcare programmes, and there are no theme parks or amusement meccas on the island.

Flora

The first explorers to land on Bermuda noted that the island was covered with an almost unbroken carpet of cedar. In the 1940s, scale insects attacked the trees, and by 1951, 85 percent of them were dead and many more were in a sad state. A reforestation programme has met with success. Bermuda cedar (a species of juniper) has been used for shipbuilding, cabinet-making, houses, and fuel.

Many of Bermuda's beautiful plants were first imported from the West Indies. The island is filled with hibiscus, morning glory (11 different species, three of them native to the island), oleander (native to Asia, and introduced into Bermuda in 1790), nasturtiums, iris, roses, bird of paradise, poinsettias, and Easter lilies among many others. The lily bulb was an important export from Bermuda in the late 1800s, but disease halted the trade in 1899. There was a revival of the Easter lily trade in the 1920s, and today a small number are exported.

It's not just the flora that's colourful

The island's profusion of shrubs include croton and lantana (called red sage elsewhere). A flowering plant called 'catch-me-if-you-can', whose leaves range from soft pink to deep rose colours, is so called because no two leaves are ever the same. The colourful Bermudiana, which is native to the island and might be called the unofficial national flower, is a small plant whose flowers have six purple petals that are yellow at the base. Bougainvillaea, a native plant of Brazil, is a climbing vine with great bursts of deep purple, salmon, red, or coral blooms.

Casuarina trees were introduced on the island to replace the cedars, there are also palmettos, royal palms, and even Norwegian pine trees. The early settlers used fronds of the Bermuda palmetto, the island's only native palm tree, to thatch their roofs. They also made a very intoxicating drink called Bibby from palmetto sap. And, in the 18th century, ladies' hats made of palmetto leaves were all the rage in London. The splendid royal poinciana (called flamboyant in the Caribbean) is a beautiful tree with showy orange-red blossoms. The olivewood bark is an endemic evergreen tree with leathery, dark green leaves and small yellowish-white flowers. The fruit of the screw pine, a tree with an unusual trunk of multiple roots, is indented like a pineapple. The sweetly scented frangipani, the yucca, and the cassia are other flowering trees.

The prickly pear is the only fruit indigenous to the island, but there are lime, lemon, tangerine, and grapefruit,

Choice fruits...

... and vegetables

as well as loquat trees. The loquat produces a yellow-orange fruit that is delicious fresh, preserved, or used as a relish or as a liqueur. Bananas are grown here, and avocados, paw-paw (papaya in the Caribbean), guavas, figs, strawberries, grapes, sweetsop, and Surinam cherries.

Bermudian farmers grow potatoes, peas, corn, lettuce, cauliflower, broccoli, and pumpkin. Onion seeds were brought to the island by early colonists, and this was the island's first crop. For many years Bermuda grew and exported onions – in fact, Bermudians came to be nicknamed 'Onions', a name that has stuck long after the vegetable ceased to be grown here. ('Him are Onions' means locally 'He's a real Bermudian!' A restaurant in Hamilton plays on the phrase, calling itself M.R. Onions.)

Birds and animals

There are no snakes in Bermuda, and no wild animals such as bears, wolves or lions. The only animal found by the first colonists was the skink, a rock lizard, and the lizard population has grown considerably. The Jamaican anole is a chameleon whose colour changes rapidly from blackish brown to green and blue; the Somerset lizard can be identified by its black eye patches, and the Warwick lizard by its yellow-gold eye ring. The giant toad – called the 'road toad', as it is often seen squashed on the road – appears in damp places, especially after rain. The nocturnal chorus heard from April to November is courtesy of the tree frogs, who sing by night and dart beneath stones or leaves by day.

Bermuda's 'national bird' is the graceful longtail, a medium-sized, satiny-white native open ocean bird with orange beak, black markings on the wings and around the eyes, and two very long central tail feathers. A perennial harbinger of spring for Bermudians, the longtail is seen swooping along the shores from March to October.

The cahow, or Bermuda petrel, is one of the world's rarest birds. It was believed extinct for 300 years until its reappearance in 1951, and is an endangered species under the protection of the Bermuda government. Some historians believe that it was the shrill cries of the cahows that frightened away early explorers and gave rise to Bermuda's ancient nickname, the 'Isles of Devils'.

The white-eyed vireo (or chick-of-the-village) is a small native bird with a cheery song which can be seen in mangroves and parks. The flamboyant kiskadee is a fly-catcher brought to Bermuda from Trinidad in 1957 to help control the lizard population. (Bermuda's lizards are probably much relieved that the kiskadee seems to prefer munching on mice, fruit, and berries.) Other colourful birds that can be seen on the island are the brilliantly-plumed cardinal, or redbird, and the eastern bluebird, a bird with a

The graceful longtail

vivid blue back and reddish-brown chest. In the autumn, migratory birds include ducks, herons, sparrows, and gulls, flocks of which can readily be seen in nature preserves such as Spittal Pond.

Of most importance to beachcombers is the wicked Portuguese man-of-war, which appears in the waters during the warm weather months. This little beastie has a myriad of tentacles that trail up to 15 metres (50ft), and will sting like the dickens if touched. Even beached specimens that appear to be dead can still sting. It is wise to read carefully the signs that are posted at beaches where you might encounter a Portuguese man-of-war. If stung by one, go immediately to the King Edward VII Memorial Hospital to get medical attention. Other beach creatures include the chiton, a flat, oval-segmented mollusc that clings tenaciously to rocks (they're known locally as 'suck rocks'), and common land crabs, which burrow deeply into south shore vegetation-covered dunes and rocky cliffs and emerge in the evening, especially after rain.

Bermuda is surrounded by an elaborate reef system, which are the most northerly of the Atlantic's reefs. Whales are occasionally spotted off the island, and dolphins can be seen in these waters. Moray eels are sometimes seen by divers, and while Bermuda waters are not exactly shark-infested, sharks are not unheard of. Other sea creatures include spiny lobster, sea horses, squid, and conch.

The pink sand for which Bermuda is so famous is made up of broken shells, pieces of coral and the calcium carbonate remains of other marine invertebrates. The pink pieces are particles of the shell of tiny single-celled animals called Foraminifera. This little creature builds a bright pink skeleton full of tiny holes through which it extends pseudopodia (infinitesimal feet) by which it attaches itself to the underside of the coral reef.

Elys Harbour and Whale Bay

Historical Highlights

C. 70,000BC Bermuda begins to emerge from a chain of volcanoes that rise from the ocean floor. Over the millennia coral shells form a 250-ft cap over the extinct volcano on which Bermuda sits.

1503AD Spanish explorer Juan de Bermudez sights the island but is frightened away by strange sounds and does not land. Bermuda's early reputation as the 'Isle of Devils' is thus established.

1511 The island La Bermuda, undoubtedly named for Bermudez, appears on a map published in the atlas *Legatio Babylonica*.

1514 Bermudez returns to the island, but is again driven away by what was probably the chattering of cahows. The legend of the Isle of Devils grows.

1515 Gonzales Ferdinando d'Oviedo makes an unsuccessful attempt to land pigs, which he thought would have provided food for survivors of possible future shipwrecks.

1543 This date, carved on a rock along with initials and a cross, is believed to have been made by Portuguese sailors, who may have shipwrecked on Bermuda in this year.

1593 Henry May, an Englishman who survived the crash of a French ship into Bermuda's reefs, provides the earliest description for English government.

1603 A Spanish galleon under the command of Diego Ramirez runs aground at Spanish Point. Ramirez dispatches some of the crew to go ashore and search for water and wood for ship repairs. The crew is also attacked by 'devils', which they discover to be birds. Ramirez makes a rough map of the island.

1609 A fleet of nine ships sails from Plymouth, England, dispatched by the Virginia Company to take supplies and settlers to the foundering British colony of Jamestown, Virginia. During a tremendous storm, the *Sea Venture*, the flagship carrying the commander of the fleet Admiral Sir George Somers and Thomas Gates, deputy governor of Jamestown, is separated from the other ships and wrecks off the northeast coast of Bermuda. The crew and passengers all survive, and come ashore in a longboat. They remain on the island for nine months, building two ships that will take them to Jamestown – the *Deliverance* and the *Patience*. Sir George explores the island and makes the first detailed map.

1610 The ships depart for Jamestown, but Sir George soon returns to Bermuda, where he dies. In Jamestown, William Strachey, Gates's secretary, writes an account of the shipwreck that is believed to have been seen by William Shakespeare and used as the basis for his play, *The Tempest*. King James I grants a charter to the Virginia Company to colonise Bermuda.

1612 *The Plough* arrives from England with 60 settlers and the first governor, Richard Moore. The first settlement is established on St George's Island, complete with fortifications. The first St Peter's Church is built, a wooden thatched-roof structure that was soon swept away by a hurricane.

1614 A Spanish galleon under the command of Domingo de Ulivari attempts to sail into Castle Harbour, but is driven away by cannon fire from the fort on Castle Island. The shot that drove the ship away was one-third of the fort's arsenal: a total of three cannonballs.

1615 Shareholders purchase the island from the Virginia Company, thus creating the Somers Island Company (also called the Bermuda Company) to oversee development of the colony.

1616 Governor Daniel Tucker succeeds Richard Moore and arrives on the *Edwin*. Richard Norwood makes the first survey and divides the island into 'tribes', now called parishes. The 'commons' is named St George's, in part for the patron saint of England and in part for Sir George, and the 'tribes' are named after investors in the Somers Company. The first black and Indian settlers arrive, possibly as slaves.

1619 The present St Peter's Church is completed.

1620 Parliament is formed, the world's second oldest after England, and meets in St Peter's Church until completion of the State House the same year.

1684 The Somers (Bermuda) Island Company is dissolved and Bermuda becomes a crown colony, administered directly by the British government.

1731 A serious epidemic of Yellow Fever.

1775 Bermudian involvement in 'The Gunpowder Plot', in which support was given to American colonists fighting War for Independence.

1784 Joseph Stockdale publishes first newspaper, the *Bermuda Gazette*.

1790 Legislation is passed to build a town that will be called Hamilton.

1809 Construction begins on Royal Naval Dockyard, using slave labour.

1814 During the War of 1812, the British launch their attack on Washington, DC, from the north shore.

1815 The capital moves from St George's to Hamilton.

1824 Convict labour arrives from Britain to help with construction of Royal Naval Dockyard.

1834 Slaves are emancipated.

1846 Gibb's Hill Lighthouse is built.

1861 The American Civil War sees Bermuda commercially active on both sides; St George's lends support to the South.

1871 On 19 September, some 6,000 people attend the opening of the Causeway, connecting the largest island with St David's, thus forging a road link between St George's and Hamilton. The Swing Bridge, between St David's and St George's islands, is part of the Causeway project.

1879 The island's second lighthouse opens on St David's Island.

1899 A tidal wave sweeps across the south coast, completely destroying the Causeway.

1901 The rebuilt Causeway reopens. The first South African Boer prisoners arrive in Bermuda. During the Boer War, thousands of prisoners are interned on islands of the Great Sound.

1902 The first Somerset versus St George's cricket 'Cup Match' is played.

1906 The Newport-Bermuda yacht race is inaugurated, hosted by the Royal Bermuda Yacht Club.

1915 The first contingent of the Bermuda Volunteer Rifle Corps goes off to World War I.

1920 The Tercentenary of Parliament is observed. The Prince of Wales visits the island, christening Somers Garden and laying the cornerstone for the Cenotaph.

1931 Inauguration of the Bermuda Railway, a narrow-gauge railroad that runs from St George's to Somerset.

1940 A base for Imperial Censorship is established at the Hamilton Princess Hotel.

1941 America begins construction of the US Naval Air Station on St David's Island. St David's, Cooper's, Longbird, and other islands are excavated and residents are relocated.

1946 Automobiles make their first appearance, bringing doom for the Bermuda Railroad.

1951 The cahow bird, thought to be extinct, is discovered in Bermuda.

1958 The wreck of the *Sea Venture* discovered.

1968 A constitution is adopted; the United Bermuda Party and Progressive Labour Party are organised.

1971 Sir Edward Richards becomes the first black Premier.

1983 Bermuda becomes a British Dependent Territory.

1985 An original Perot Stamp, Bermuda's first postage stamp, sells for nearly $60,000.

1995 A referendum on whether Bermuda should secede from the British Commonwealth fails. The US Naval Air Station closes.

1997 Pamela Gordon is the first woman to be elected Premier. The Bermuda Underwater Exploration Institute opens.

Previous pages: sailboats, Mangrove Bay and Hamilton (above)
Pastel frontage on Front Street

Gombey dancers

Route 1

Tour of Hamilton, the Capital *See map on page 19*

Hamilton, Bermuda's capital, sits on a gently sloping hill above a picturesque harbour. Front Street, its main street, bustles with small cars, mopeds, and buses that tool past downtown's balconied and arcaded buildings. Hamilton is a small town; fewer than 2,000 people reside in the capital. There are no skyscrapers or neon signs, no trolleys and certainly no subways. At one time a railroad ran smack down the middle of Front Street, but that all changed in 1946 with the arrival of the first automobiles on the island.

The tower of the Bermuda Cathedral soars above the pastel-coloured buildings, most of them no more than two or three storeys high, and dominates the skyline. The tower is easily seen from Paget and Warwick parishes across the harbour.

On the water side of Front Street, sightseeing boats dock to take on passengers for trips around the harbour and across the Great Sound. Ferry boats churn back and forth across the harbour, carrying commuters and tourists to and from Paget, Warwick, and Somerset parishes. The harbour is lined with pink buildings, called locally sheds, that house Customs and other administrative offices. In No. 1 Shed, during the low season, between November and March, weekly fashion shows, teas, and performances of the island's unique Gombey Dancers are held. And from April until October, in high season, sleek luxury liners ease into the harbour and dock here, letting their passengers loose for shopping sprees and sightseeing tours. During that time, Wednesday nights are Harbour Nights, when Hamilton's streets are filled with food booths, music, and milling crowds, and the shops stay open late.

As the capital, Hamilton is home to the houses of parliament and to administrative offices, but for visitors the town's premier attractions are its shops. Bermuda shopkeepers purchase directly from European manufacturers, and for US travellers there are substantial discounts here on everything from woollens and luxury cashmere to cameras and wristwatches.

Shops are a main attraction

A tour of Hamilton should properly begin at the **Visitors Bureau** ❶ (8 Front St, tel: 295-1480; 9am–4pm April–October, 9am–2pm November–March, closed Sundays year-round) in the Ferry Terminal Building for maps, brochures, and plenty of friendly advice. Upon leaving the Ferry Terminal, turn left and walk down Point Pleasant Road to a little park called ★ **Albuoys Point** ❷. From here there is a lovely view of Hamilton Harbour, with its deep blue waters dotted with small islands, and its graceful sailboats, slow-moving ferries and, in high season, majestic luxury liners. To your left as you look out over the harbour is the private Royal Bermuda Yacht Club, which was built in 1930; the club itself was organised in 1844. Needless to say, the yacht club plays a major role in Bermuda's various races on the seas.

Backtrack up Point Pleasant Road, cross Front Street and turn right. In the middle of the street, you'll see the ★ **Birdcage** ❸, in which police sometimes direct

The Birdcage

Shoppers paradise

Fascinating Bermudiana

Moon gate at Par-la-Ville

traffic – usually only during high season, and for tourists' photo opportunities. Walk past the Irish Linen Shop – a good place to visit if you're interested in anything from dishcloths to christening gowns. You'll pass the Bermuda Book Store, which, among other books, is filled with volumes focusing on Bermuda. Near at hand on Front Street are the ages-old department stores, Trimingham's and H.A.&E. Smith's – wonderful places to browse around if you're a serious shopper.

Turn left on Queen Street, continuing to the ★★ **Perot Post Office** ❹ (tel: 292-9052; 9am–5pm, closed Saturday and Sunday). This little branch of the post office is named for William Bennet Perot, Bermuda's first postmaster, who was appointed in 1818. The building dates from 1840, and has a rather Pickwickian flavour. Perot is credited with creating Bermuda's first book of stamps, and the first postmaster's stamps are now rare and highly prized collectors' items.

A few steps beyond the post office is the original Perot family home, a Georgian building that now houses the ★★ **Museum of the Bermuda Historical Society and the Bermuda Library** ❺ (tel: 295-2487; 9.30am–3.30pm, closed Sunday). The museum holds a fascinating collection of Bermudiana, including Sir George Somers' lodestone; portraits of Sir George and his wife, of the Perots, and of the original Bermuda Company investors; ancient coins and antique cedar furnishings; early 17th-century maps of the island, and a letter from George Washington, written in 1775 to request Bermuda's help in the US War for Independence from England. Washington's letter is in the archives, but not on display.

There is also a plaster-of-Paris mould of Spanish Rock – a block of stone found by early settlers in Spittal Pond, crudely carved with letters and numerals. Historians believe that a Portuguese ship landed here in the year 1543, and the rock markings were carved by the ship's sailors. In addition to loaning books, the Bermuda Library has a collection of rare 17th-century books and newspapers that date back to 1787.

Between the Historical Society and the Perot Post Office is the entrance to ★ **Par-la-Ville Park** ❻, which was the 19th-century garden in which postmaster Perot liked to play putt. (The huge rubber tree in front of the museum, sent to Mr. Perot from what is now Guyana, was planted by the postmaster in 1847.) Landscaped with green lawns, lush plants and decorated with stone moon gates – popular in gardens all over the islands – the idyllic park is often crowded around noontime with office workers who enjoy taking time out for a spot of lunch or simply to catch the sun's rays on the park benches.

In front of the Perot Post Office is the intersection of

Queen Street and Reid Street. Bluck's, on the corner, is
a very elegant store that purveys fine china and crystal
at substantial discounts. A few steps away on the same
side of the street, the Phoenix Centre is handy to know
about, with a pharmacy, newsstand, film, and sundries.
Cross Queen Street and turn left to cut through Washington Lane to Church Street. ★★ **Hamilton City Hall** **❼**
(tel: 292-1234; 9am–5pm, closed Saturday and Sunday),
a handsome whitewashed Bermuda-style edifice, is topped
by a tall tower with a weathervane that's shaped like the
ill-fated *Sea Venture*, the shipwreck of which led to the
colonisation of Bermuda.

Sea Venture atop City Hall

In addition to housing administrative offices, City Hall
is home to the **Bermuda National Gallery** (tel: 295-
9428), of which Bermudians are justifiably proud, as well
as the galleries and exhibits of the **Bermuda Society of
Arts** (tel: 292-3824), and a theatre. Local productions
are often mounted in the City Hall Theatre, but this is
also a major venue for the Bermuda Festival, held each
year between January and March, which draws inter-
nationally renowned performers for its programmes of
dramatic plays, music, and dance.

21

Turn left after leaving City Hall and walk a half block
along Church Street to Washington Street, which is the terminal for the pink-and-blue buses that criss-cross the island. You may want to hold your breath to avoid gulping
fumes, but the kiosk here is where you buy books of tickets and visitors passes for the buses and ferries.

Continue one block to Victoria Street to see ★ **Victoria
Park** **❽**, with its Victorian bandstand and sunken gardens. During the summer, concerts are sometimes held
in the landscaped park. The park was dedicated to Queen
Victoria in honour on the occasion of her Golden Jubilee.

Bordering Victoria Park on the east side is Cedar

Pretty Victoria Park

Most Holy Trinity
In the pink – St Andrew's

Avenue. If you followed the avenue on out past St Theresa's Catholic Church and beyond, you'd come to the Government Tennis Stadium, which is open to visitors. And at nearby Bernard Park there are regularly scheduled cricket, soccer, and softball games, at which spectators are welcome. Cedar Avenue continues northwards through the Black Watch Pass (see Route 2, page 27) and connects with North Shore Road.

Backtrack along Washington Street to Church Street and turn left to reach the ★★★ **Church of the Most Holy Trinity ❾** – the Anglican church, usually referred to locally as the Bermuda Cathedral. The imposing building is the second church to occupy this site, the first, built in 1872, having been destroyed by an arsonist. The present Restoration gothic church was designed by William Hay of Edinburgh, built with materials imported from all over the globe, and completed in 1911. The impressive interior includes carved English oak, Italian marble, and beautiful stained-glass windows. The 157 steps lead up to the tower (10am–4pm, closed Saturday and Sunday), which affords a panoramic view.

Other nearby religious edifices, on and around aptly-named Church Street, are the Wesley Methodist Church, St Theresa's Catholic Church (seat of the island's six Catholic churches), the Muslim Community Center, a Christian Science Church and Reading Room, and **St Andrew's Presbyterian Church ❿** (the island's oldest church, erected in 1846).

From the Bermuda Cathedral, turn left and cross Church Street, then stroll along one block and turn right on Parliament Street. En route you'll pass the main post office. The dramatic structure across from you in Parliament

Sessions House

Street is ★★ **Sessions House ⓫** (tel: 292-7408; 9am–

12.30pm and 2–5pm, closed Saturday and Sunday), in which the House of Assembly debates and the Supreme Court deliberates. The building dates from 1817, but its most spectacular aspects – the terracotta ornamentation and Italianate towers – were added in 1887, the year of Queen Victoria's Golden Jubilee. When the House of Assembly is in session, the visitors gallery is also open to the public, and you can observe the parliamentary participants, garbed in wigs and gowns just as in the mother country, England.

Home to the Cabinet

After leaving Sessions House, continue walking along Parliament Street towards the harbour. The ★★ **Cabinet Building ⑫** (tel: 292-5501, 9am–5pm, closed Saturday and Sunday), where the lower house of parliament convenes, occupies the entire block between Reid and Front Street. Dating from 1833, the Cabinet Building houses the Premier's offices, as well as the hall in which the Cabinet and the Senate meet. On the first Friday in November, this 19th-century building is the site of colourful ceremonies for the Convening of Parliament, when the Governor, his spiffy attire topped by a plumed helmet, arrives in a horse-drawn carriage. With much pomp and pageantry the meeting is called to order, after which the Governor addresses those assembled from a small 17th-century cedar 'throne.'

23

In front of the Cabinet Building, the ★ **Cenotaph ⑬**, modelled on the one in Whitehall in London, is a limestone monument commemorating Bermuda's war dead. In 1920, on the island's Tercentenary, the cornerstone for the Cenotaph was laid by the Prince of Wales on one of his several goodwill tours.

The Fort's for skirling

On Happy Valley Road, on the outskirts east of the capital, ★★★ **Fort Hamilton ⑭** (tel: 292-2845, 9.30am–4pm) is an imposing old party that was constructed in 1889. Replete with moats and dungeons and guns (which have never been fired in anger), this fortress is one of several constructed by order of the Duke of Wellington. At noon each Monday, from November through March, visitors can watch a Skirling Ceremony performed by the Bermuda Isles Pipe Band and Dancers, dressed in traditional kilts. Usually, one of the pipers plays a soul-stirring rendition of *Amazing Grace*, and the band marches smartly off the green to the rousing tune of 'Scotland, the Brave.' In addition to the pageantry, Fort Hamilton offers visitors picture-postcard views of the capital, its harbour, and the surrounding area. There is also a tearoom at the fort – but don't even think about trying to get into the little place for a quick drink and a snack immediately following the ceremony.

ATLANTIC OCEAN

Daniel's
Island

Daniel's
Head

Somerset
Long Bay

Long Bay
Nature
Reserve

Cambridge
Beaches

Mangrove
Bay

Ireland Island
South

Commissi
House
Ireland Island
North

Royal Navy
Cemetery

Boaz
Is.

Lagoon
Park

Somerset
Village

Springfield

Gilbert Nature
Reserve

Watford
Bridge

Watford
Is.

Scotts Hill Road

St James
Church

Heydon
Trust
Estate

Plaice's
Point

Cavello
Bay

Somerset
Island

Scaur Hill
Fort Park

Great
Sound

Somerset
Road

Ely's Harbour

Railway Trail

Somerset
Bridge

Wreck Road

Overplus
Lane

Hawkins
Is.

Lo

Railway Trail

Former
US Naval
Station
Annex

Little
Sound

Burt's
Is.

Darrell's Is.

Pompano
Beach Club

Port Royal
Golf Course

Evans
Bay

West Whale
Bay Fort

Frank's
Bay

Perot's
Is.

Riddell's Bay
Golf Course

Burnt House Hill Rd

Bermuda
Triangle Brewery

Bermuda
Golf Academy

Middle Road

Riddells Bay Road

Mid

Railway Trail

Gibbs Hill
Lighthouse

Church
Bay

Princess
Golf Course

Sonesta
Beach Resort

Horseshoe
Bay

Chaplin
Bay

Warwick
Long Ba

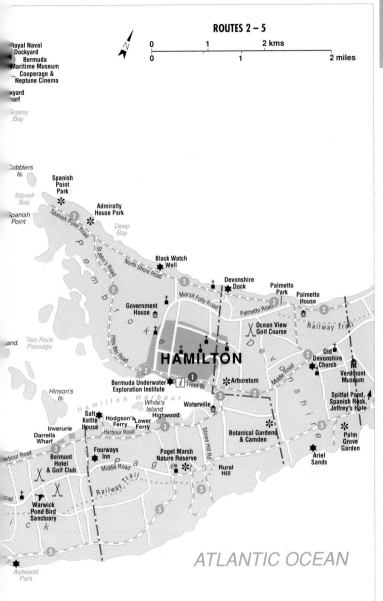

ROUTES 2 – 5

Royal Naval
Dockyard
Bermuda
Maritime Museum
Cooperage &
Neptune Cinema
ckyard
harf
Grassy
Bay

Cobblers
Is.

Stovell
Bay

Spanish
Point

Spanish
Point
Park

Admiralty
House Park

Deep
Bay

Spanish Point Road

St John's Road

North Shore Road

Black Watch
Well

Devonshire
Dock

Marsh Folly Road

Palmetto
Park

Palmetto Road

Palmetto
House

Railway Trail

Government
House

P   e   m   b   r   o   k   e

Pitts Bay Road

HAMILTON

Ocean View
Golf Course

Two Rock
Passage

land.

Hinson's
Is.

Bermuda Underwater
Exploration Institute

Front St

Arboretum

Old
Devonshire
Church

Verdmont
Museum

Spittal Pond,
Spanish Rock,
Jeffrey's Hole

Middle Road

D   e   v   o   n   s   h   i   r   e

Hamilton   Harbour

White's
Island

Highwood

Waterville

Salt
Kettle
House

Hodgson's
Ferry

Lower
Ferry

Harbour Road

Stowe Hill Rd.

Botanical Gardens
& Camden

Palm
Grove
Garden

Inverurie
Darrells
Wharf

arbour Road

Belmont
Hotel
& Golf Club

Fourways
Inn

Middle Road

Paget Marsh
Nature Reserve

Rural
Hill

Ariel
Sands

P   a   g   e   t

Railway Trail

oad

Warwick
Pond Bird
Sanctuary

W   a   r   w   i   c   k

Astwood
Park

ATLANTIC OCEAN

Inside Old Devonshire Church

Route 2

Hamilton's Environs *See map on pages 24–25*

Tour of Pembroke Parish, west of the town of Hamilton, along North Shore Road and via Middle Road to the Old Devonshire Church, ending at the Arboretum.

While Hamilton and the town of St George can easily be toured on foot, you'll need a moped for this and other tours of the island.

Depart Hamilton, headed west on Pitts Bay Road, which is the westward extension of Front Street. Continue northwest on Pitts Bay Road. Heading out this way you'll pass Waterloo House, a very elegant small hotel whose white-columned frontage overlooks the harbour. Its charming entrance, has a patio filled with flowering plants. It was built around the turn of the 18th century as a private home, and the name was changed to Waterloo in honour of Wellington's defeat of Napoleon in 1815. A lot of construction work has been going on a little past Waterloo House. The huge Bermudiana Hotel has been razed, leaving an enormous hole. An executive office building will replace it, and another such building site is across the street – much to the chagrin of Waterloo House and the adjacent Hamilton Princess, Bermuda's grande dame hotel. This hotel was built in 1884, and is credited with kicking off tourism on the island. Across the street from the Princess, sitting on a hill amid manicured lawns, is Rosedon, once a private estate and now a pleasant guest house.

A Waterloo House welcome Hamilton's grande dame hotel

Follow Pitts Bay Road and turn left on St John's Road, which eventually merges with Spanish Point Road. On the right is ★ **Admiralty House Park**, a 6-hectare (16-acre) park with its picturesque coves and caves. In the mid-19th

century, this was the home of the commander of the naval base at Dockyard. The house has long since been demolished, but in any case the attraction here is the sheltered cove and the beach. This is a pleasant spot for picnicking and lazing away an hour or two.

Continuing west you'll come to ★ **Spanish Point Park**, where there are the remains of a huge floating dockyard, now reminiscent of a whale skeleton. The floating dock once did yeoman service when it was anchored at the Royal Naval Dockyard. The little park here is not very inspirational, but there is a peaceful beach.

Spanish Point Park with a beach

Backtrack on Spanish Point Road, which becomes North Shore Road, and ★ **Langton Hill** will presently loom up on your right. Atop the hill is Government House, the home to Bermuda's governor, which is not open to the public. Completed in 1892, Government House has been the scene of numerous state occasions, with distinguished visitors including Queen Elizabeth II and Prince Philip. It has long been the custom for visiting dignitaries and heads of state to plant a tree, and the grounds are shaded with those planted by at least two Princes of Wales and Queen Elizabeth II, as well as by Ethiopia's Emperor Haile Selassie. In 1973, the grounds were the scene of a brutal murder, when Governor Richard Sharples was assassinated, along with his bodyguard, Captain Hugh Sayers. The assassin was later executed; Sharples and Sayers are buried side by side in St Peter's Churchyard.

27

A short distance from Langton Hill, coming up on your right is the ★★ **Black Watch Well** and **Black Watch Pass**. The well, long-since capped, was dug in 1849 by the Bermuda regiment of the famed Black Watch on orders of the Governor, in order to alleviate the suffering of local residents in this area during a severe drought. To create Black Watch Pass, which is named for the well, the Public Works Department had to cut out more than 2½ million cubic feet of solid limestone, an awesome feat, indeed. The tunnel-like passageway connects North Shore Drive with Cedar Avenue in Hamilton (*see Route 1*), and with Marsh Folly Road. The name Marsh Folly comes from the considerable funds squandered in 1934 in the plan to reclaim Pembroke Marsh into a racetrack and recreation area. In the Town of St George, there is a Church Folly Lane, also named for a large expenditure of money.

Black Watch Well

Incidentally, it was on the northern coast, just opposite where the Black Watch Well was built, that was the location of the infamous Ducking Stool. A replica of the seesaw-resembling device is on display in King's Square in St George's, and is occasionally used, all in fun, for demonstrations for tourists. But the original Ducking Stool was used, for real, in the colony's early days to punish 'nagging wives and gossips', and other perceived

Catch of the day at Devonshire

Old Devonshire Church of limestone
Trees from all over the world

malefactors. The offending lady was made to sit on the stool and then was dunked in the waters, presumably to cleanse her of her irritating ways.

Drive along North Shore Road and you'll see on your left ★ **Devonshire Dock**, a picturesque spot where fishermen haul in the day's catch. Needless to say, the views of the blue ocean waters are spectacular. Across the traffic island at Barkers Hill Road you'll come to a large expanse of green called Palmetto Park, and just beyond it, ★ **Palmetto House** (tel:236-6483, Bermuda National Trust; 10am–5pm Thursday only), an early 18th-century cruciform house (a structure believed to be built in the shape of a cross). Some fine examples of Bermudian cedar furniture can be seen in the three rooms of the house that are open for tours.

Straight ahead on North Shore Road is the waterside Clayhouse Inn, a venerable and very popular nightclub that features a rousing show of calypso music and limbo dancers – a place you may want to tuck away in your memory bank for future reference.

Backtrack along the main road and turn left on busy Barker's Hill Road, which connects with Middle Road. The road whips past 9-hole Ocean View Golf Course, one of the three government-run courses. To your left, on Vesey Street, is the National Equestrian Centre, where numerous horse shows are held. Devonshire Marsh at Middle Road, is a 4-hectare (10-acre) untamed marsh, whose wilds are protected by the Bermuda Audubon Society.

Turn left on Middle Road to the ★★ **Old Devonshire Church** (tel: 236-3671; open daily). This is the second church to sit on this site; the first one, erected in 1623, was blown away by a hurricane. The first church is believed to have been of limestone with a thatched roof; it was one of four churches built that year. Its replacement was completed in 1716, though it was not consecrated until April 13, 1826. The present church was damaged by an explosion on Easter Sunday 1970. The little white limestone building looks for all the world like a Bermuda cottage. Among its treasures are a silver communion cup, bearing a 1590 hallmark, that was bequeathed to the church by Captain Roger Wood, who served as governor from 1629 until 1637. Services are held in the nearby Christ Church, the 'new' parish church that was completed in 1851.

Turn left after leaving the church and go along Middle Road to the ★★ **Arboretum** (open sunrise to sunset daily), a 8-hectare (20-acre) tract of lovely trees, not all of which are indigenous to the island. Developed for experimental purposes, the arboretum has been planted with trees from all over the world, to ascertain which can survive in Bermuda's humid semitropical climate.

Return to Hamilton along Middle Road.

Route 3

Tour of Harbour Road *See map on pages 24–25*

This tour, which goes through Paget, Warwick, and Southampton parishes, begins at the Bermuda Underwater Exploration Institute and continues along Harbour Road and Middle Road to Somerset Bridge.

Depart Hamilton heading east on Front Street, which becomes East Broadway as it edges around Hamilton Harbour. The ★★★ **Bermuda Underwater Exploration Institute** (tel: 292-7219, 10am–6pm), which sits right on the edge of the water, was completed in the summer of 1997, and is one of the island's stellar attractions. The 3,700-sq. metre (40,000-sq. ft) state-of-the-art Institute, also called BUEI – designed to 'amaze, excite, inform, and inspire' – has among its exhibits those that examine Bermuda's volcanic origins, the island's extensive reef system, and the creatures that inhabit the waters in which the island sits.

There are numerous computer-generated interactive exhibits, and a simulated dive 3,700 metres (12,000ft) to the ocean floor. To take the 'dive', you enter a 'capsule' in which the sounds and sensations of a watery descent are simulated. The capsule is actually an elevator, and the dive is to the basement, where there are more exhibits and simulations, but it is all nevertheless effective. In addition to the obligatory gift shop, there is an excellent restaurant overlooking the harbour and dining inside or al fresco.

Upon leaving the BUEI, turn right and continue to the first roundabout, the Crow Lane traffic circle. If you happen to come along this way any weekday from 5am until about 10am, you'll see Johnny Barnes, waving, blowing kisses, and bidding all passers-by a 'Good Morning. Have

Spoils from the sea

29

Underwater Exploration Institute

Johnny preserved for posterity

Candy-coloured home

a good day!' Barnes, a retired bus driver, is an island institution. In the summer of 1998, the gregarious septuagenarian travelled to London to pose for a sculptor; the resulting statue has pride of place in the traffic circle.

A left turn at the traffic circle would take you to Point Finger Road, and the King Edward VII Memorial Hospital, Bermuda's modern medical facility. However, hopefully you've no immediate need for medical attention, so turn right at the roundabout and drive along Harbour Road.

Harbour Road is a lovely drive, lined with handsome houses. The drive follows the contours of the harbour and there are some splendid vistas of the water and Hamilton, but houses, shops, and trees line the road all along the way, obscuring the view. To get right on the water you have to take the little lanes and alleys off to the right (as you travel west), some of which lead to the landings for the little ferries that churn to and fro across the harbour.

A few minutes after turning on Harbour Road you'll notice on your right a house called **Waterville** (tel: 236-6483, offices open Monday–Friday 9am–5pm, gift shop open Monday–Saturday 9am–4pm), which contains the offices of the **Bermuda National Trust**. The Trust is charged with restoring and preserving many of the island's historic buildings, gardens, and open spaces. Proceeds from the 'Trustworthy' gift shop here are used for Trust projects. In a somewhat bucolic setting, albeit right on a main road, 'Waterville' is a lovely 18th-century house that was the Trimingham family home. (You may have noticed in this area Trimingham Drive, Trimingham Road, and Trimingham Hill. Locals sometimes refer to the Crow Lane roundabout as the Trimingham traffic circle.) The drawing room and dining room of the house can be seen during business hours.

View from Somerset Bridge

The street that runs alongside Waterville – Pomander Road – leads to the Pomander Gate Tennis Club, where the Pomander Gate Tennis Open is held every year in June. Across the street is the charming Little Pomander Guest House, which sits smack on the harbour.

Back on Harbour Road, look to your left just past Lovers Lane to see the rambling house on the hill, festooned with lovely woodwork. The 19th-century home of Sir Brown-low Gray, Chief Justice of Bermuda, this was the first house on the island to have a tennis court – some say it was the first court in the Western Hemisphere – and it was from here that tennis was introduced into the United States.

In 1873, a Bermudian gentleman returned from a visit to England, bringing with him all the accoutrements of lawn tennis, which was at that time all the rage in Britain. But when it dawned on him, to his horror, that in order to play the game his wife would actually have to run – most undignified behaviour for a lady – he gave all of the equipment to Mr Gray, who then built the tennis court where all of his family learned to play. In 1874, Miss Mary Outer-bridge, visiting Bermuda from the United States, is said to have learned to play the game on the courts of this house, and upon her return to New York she took with her a rules book and racquets and requested that the Staten Island Cricket Club build a tennis court.

31

Opposite Highwood Lane, just past Clermont, is the ferry landing called Lower Ferry. When ferry service across the harbour began here in 1818, passengers were ferried in rowboats – a mode of transportation that continued into the 1940s.

The island you can see from here is White's Island. There is little to be seen there now, but around the turn of the 20th century a biologist from New York University used the island as a base for his shipments of live Bermuda fish to the New York Aquarium, and in 1917–18, the US Navy had a base on the island.

Continuing on Harbour Road, coming up on your right is Newstead, a very elegant Relais et Châteaux that is in a great location. Steps behind Newstead's tennis courts lead down to Hodson's Ferry and a five-minute ride over the harbour to Hamilton.

View over Salt Kettle Bay

Further along, Salt Kettle Road noses out into the harbour on a peninsula, past Mrs Hazel Lowe's delightful Salt Kettle Guest House, and Salt Kettle Boat Rentals, where you can rent yachts, powerboats, and sailboats, and to the Salt Kettle Ferry Landing. Salt Kettle was one of the first settlements on this part of the harbour. The name 'Salt Kettle' comes from the early days of the colony when salt was extracted from sea water in salt kettles. Not long after Hamilton was incorporated in 1790, rowboats began a ferry service to the settlement, and in 1794, passengers were ferried twice weekly from here to St George's in a sailboat known as the *Salt Kettle Stage*. In 1867, the *Express* – a small steamboat – began a ferry service, and for the first several days after its inauguration hundreds of passengers are said to have packed the boat to enjoy the breezy new ride across Hamilton Harbour.

The property you see sitting on Salt Kettle Bay is the former Inverurie Hotel, a 19th-century house that opened as a hotel in 1910. It changed hands in 1990, closed for good a few years later, and is destined to become condominiums. It seems a great pity that it no longer exists, as the Inverurie was almost legendary.

Opposite the erstwhile Inverurie, the road leading up the hill is Cobb's Hill Road which cuts from north to south across the island and is the dividing line between Paget and Warwick parishes. At the top, at the intersection of Middle Road, is Fourways Inn, one of the island's loveliest hotels and a member of the Small Luxury Hotels of the World. The main building, in which an elegant Sunday brunch is served, was an inn during the 18th century, and the kitchen produces luscious goodies for the Fourways Pastry Shop in the Washington Mall in Hamilton.

Flying the flag
Golfers stop at Belmont

Down on the water below the old Inverurie is the ferry landing Darrell's Wharf, which is named for a prominent family whose private dock this was in earlier times. Darrell's Island lying to the west of the harbour is named for the same family. The large island near the coast is the privately-owned Hinson's Island. The first airplane to arrive in Bermuda landed on this island in 1919, brought here by two veterans of World War I. The two aviators began the short-lived Bermuda and West Atlantic Aviation Company, with headquarters on Hinson's Island. The company foundered, as it was too far ahead of its time. Bermuda's first airport was on Darrell's Island, and remained there until after World War II, when Kindley Field opened on St George's Island.

The next ferry stop on the water below Harbour Road is Belmont Wharf, and above it, sitting on a hill, is the Belmont Hotel and Golf Club which has entrances off both Harbour Road and Middle Road. This hotel is a great favourite among golfers, as it has one of the island's popular golf courses.

The road continues along the harbour and merges with the curiously named Burnt House Hill Road. The name comes from olden days, when many houses in this area were burned down to get rid of a plague of rats! Riddell's Bay is west of Burnt House Hill Road. The government-owned Riddell's Bay Golf Course is the oldest golf course on the island.

At Riddell's Bay, Burnt House Hill Road merges with Middle Road, which continues under various aliases all the way out to Royal Naval Dockyard (*see Route 4*). South of where the two roads merge are Warwick Long Bay and Horseshoe Bay, with some of the island's prettiest beaches (*see Route 7*). Not far past where Middle and Burnt House Hill Road merge, South Road swoops up and also becomes one with Middle Road. Beyond this point, look on your right for the entrance to the Waterlot Inn, which sits on a picturesque bay. An inn during the 17th century, this cottage is now a very fine restaurant, one of several eateries owned by the Southampton Princess Hotel. Keep Waterlot in mind if wooing your sweetheart is on your mind, as it's a very romantic, if pricey, place for dinner by candlelight.

Golf at the Academy

A short distance from where South Road merges with Middle Road, look for Granaway Heights Road on the left, and past it Industrial Park Road. Turn left there and drive down to the ★ **Bermuda Golf Academy** (tel: 238-8800; 8am–11pm), which is a very golf-orientated place. There is a 320-yard driving range with 40 practice bays (25 of them covered), an 18-hole practice green, eight target greens, a practise chipping and bunker play area, and a mini-golf area. You can take golf instruction here, get your clubs repaired, and rent clubs if you don't happen to have any with you. There is even a children's play area and a restaurant, where big-screen TVs show continuous videos of – what else? – golfing events. The place is lit up like a Christmas tree until 10.30pm.

Further along on the same road, the ★ **Bermuda Triangle Brewery** (tel: 238-2430; tours at 4pm Saturday the year round, and at 4pm Monday–Friday March–October) is Bermuda's first microbrewery, and

33

Get lost in the Bermuda Triangle

offers free tours and samples. As indicated by the name of the road on which you came, this is an industrial centre with a cement plants, a quarry, and a cluster of warehouses. The brewery is across from Ace Hardware, and while it isn't much to look at, this is not meant to be a feast for the eyes. The proof of the pudding is in the tasting, or in this case the proof of the beer, and after learning how the beer is brewed you can have a taste of Hammerhead stout, Wilde Hogg Amber Ale, Spinnaker pilsner, and Full Moon pale ale – 'brewed only in the light of the full moon'.

A short distance along Middle Road, long, winding Whale Bay Road leads out to the ruins of the small **Whale Bay Fort** (open space, always accessible). Actually, the road itself does not lead to the fort: it takes you to the point where you can abandon your moped and walk down a grassy sloping hill. There isn't much left of the 19th-century fort, and the small white-sand beach here disappears and reappears with the tide. It is a nice sheltered beach, though, when it's there. At the top of the hill, the Whale Bay Inn has five small but very charmingly furnished apartments.

Port Royal green

34

The front lawn of Whale Bay Inn overlooks the ★★**Port Royal Golf Club** (tel: 234-0974), which will hove into view your left as you continue driving along Middle Road. The club and its facilities, including an 18-hole golf course, tennis courts, and a restaurant, are open to the public.

Across Middle Road from Port Royal, jutting out into the Great Sound, is the former US Naval Station Annexe. The air station closed in 1995 and, at the time of going to press, various ideas about building a public golf course on this site were being bandied about. The peninsula on which the annexe sat was once two islands, which were joined together to create the peninsula. These are

The beach at Whale Bay

just two of the more than 100 islands in the Great Sound, some of them privately owned.

Sally-Anne waits, Somerset

Just past the golf course, on your left Pompano Road is another long paved road that will take you down to the Pompano Beach Club, a great place to stay, especially if you're keen on water sports. It's owned by two Americans, Tom and Larry Lamb, and when it opened in 1956 it was the island's first fishing club. There's a good restaurant, outstanding water sports facilities, and spectacular views when the sun sinks down into the water.

In this area the Railway Trail (*see pages 68–9*) runs parallel to Middle Road. If you've come this far you're no doubt on wheels, and vehicles are not allowed along this portion of the trail. But keep this place in mind for possible future exploration, as the trail wanders along some beautiful bays of the Great Sound. Evans Pond, a wintertime roost for herons, lies beside a hillside that's covered with cedar trees and flowers. The pond and Evans Bay Wharf on the Great Sound were named for a family of that name that once lived in this area.

Coming up on your right is a short street, Overplus Lane, whose odd name dates from the island's first survey in 1616. When Sir Richard Norwood surveyed the island and divided it into 'tribes' (now called parishes), he was directed by the then-Governor Daniel Tucker to locate a prime piece of real estate. Tucker had been promised by the Somers Island Company a bonus for his work as governor, and when Norwood described this particular part of the island he decided that this was to be his reward. Norwood omitted from his survey lands in this area, just as if it did not exist. Tucker then claimed 80 hectares (200 acres), a much larger piece of land than had been promised him, and without waiting for the Somers Island Company's investors to approve of the deal he immediately proceeded to build a fine house for himself on it. Tucker's scheme was found out, and the upshot of the matter was the 'overplus' was divided between Southampton and Sandys parishes, with the greater portion going to the latter.

35

The world's smallest drawbridge

You'll soon cross ★★ **Somerset Bridge**, reportedly one of the world's smallest drawbridges (just 76 cms/30 inches, enough for a ship's mast to pass through). Historical records reveal that this bridge was here as early as 1620. It's very tiny, and unless you're looking for it, and notice the different sound your tyres make when they briefly leave paved road and hit the wooden bridge, you'll scarcely know you crossed it.

There is a ferry landing at Somerset Bridge, and at this point you can board the ferry and return to Hamilton, or continue on the tour described in the following Route 4.

Pirates haven

Route 4

Somerset and Royal Naval Dockyard, via ferry from Hamilton *See map on pages 24–25*

Bermuda, of course, is not one island, but an archipelago comprising more than 150 islands. But because of the connecting bridges you have very little sense of crossing from island to island. This tour traverses the four islands which constitute the so-called 'West End'. The main one, Somerset, derives its name from Admiral Sir George Somers; although the survivors of the 1609 wreck of his flagship the *Sea Venture* swam ashore at the East End, during his sojourn Sir George was drawn to this island in the west, and it became known as "Somers' seate". It was the wreck of the *Sea Venture* which led to the colonisation of Bermuda.

The tour begins in Hamilton, at the Ferry Terminal on Front Street, where you'll board the Somerset Ferry. Mopeds will be necessary, and can be taken aboard the Somerset Ferry. Note on the ferry schedule that one of the ferry routes goes directly to Royal Naval Dockyard, a trip of an hour and 15 minutes. For the tour, take care that you board the ferry that goes to Somerset Bridge, and get off there. You can return to Hamilton from Dockyard, but make sure you note the departure time for the ferry. On Sundays, the last boat leaves Dockyard at 5.30pm and arrives in Hamilton at 6.45pm.

View over Elys Harbour

Just across Somerset Bridge is beautiful ★★★ **Ely's Harbour**. Pronounced *Ee-lee*, this harbour was named after a William Ely, who lived here in 1621. The peaceful port, with small fishing boats bobbing on the water, was once a haven for smugglers.

There are several places around here named Wreck – Wreck Hill, Wreck Road, and Wreck Bay. The name goes all the way back to 1618 and the Flemish Wreck – the ruin of the Dutch frigate was the first recorded after the wreck of the *Sea Venture*.

On this side of Somerset Bridge, Middle Road becomes Somerset Road, and a bit further along, ★★ **Scaur Hill Fort Park** (9am–4pm), on the right, is a pretty park with the remains of another of Bermuda's many fortifications, along with splendid vistas of the Sound. Somerset Road is a beautiful scenic drive, but there are some hair-raising curves along the way.

Scaur Hill Fort views

Not far from Scaur Hill you'll see Willowbank Guest House, on a promontory overlooking Ely's Harbour. A quiet hotel where grace is said before each meal and morning devotionals are held. It offers an alternative to the big splashy resort properties.

Just across the road from Willowbank – and you have to look sharp or you'll miss it, there is no blinking neon sign here (or anywhere else on the island) – is the entrance to the large 17-hectare (43-acre) ★★ **Heydon Trust Estate** (tel: 234-1831). Awash with citrus groves, banana trees, and bird sanctuaries, the private estate is maintained in an undeveloped state as a reminder of what Bermuda was like in the early days of the colony. It is indeed quiet and peaceful, with park benches and beautiful vistas of the Great Sound. The tiny chapel dates from before 1620, and services are still held here. Just outside the chapel you can look across the water to see the peninsula on which the US Naval Air Station Annexe used to be.

Services are still held in the chapel

Continuing along Somerset Road you'll see on your left the **St James Anglican Church**, a lovely building which was consecrated in 1789. In 1937, the graceful spire, added in 1880, crashed down into the centre aisle of the church. The present spire is a replica, erected shortly thereafter.

Nearby is the **Somerset Visitors Bureau** (tel: 234-1388), which is only open between April and November, during high season. Past the Visitors Bureau you'll cross Hook 'n' Ladder Lane (another of Bermuda's streets with a name straight out of a storybook). Look on your right for Springfield and the Gilbert Nature Reserve, properties of the Bermuda National Trust. Springfield was a private estate in the 1700s, and is named for the family who lived there. It later became a branch of the Bermuda Public Library. At press time it was closed for restoration. The wooded Anita Wingate Trail wanders for a half-mile through the nature reserve.

Gateway to St James

Somerset Road makes a sharp right turn at the junction of Cambridge Road, and continues to sleepy ★ **Somerset Village**, where it comes to an end at Mangrove Bay Road.

Picture-perfect Mangrove Bay

Stunning view at Cavello Bay

Long Bay for sun worshippers

Take time to wander through the village, which is entirely different from Hamilton and St George's. Like Flatts, it's quite small and has the feel of a little country village. (Bermudians refer to anything outside of Hamilton as being 'out in the country'.) The Somerset Bus Terminal in 'downtown Somerset' was the western terminal for the narrow-gauge Bermuda Railway (*see pages 68–9*). Some of the Hamilton shops have branches here, and they too have a rural aura about them.

From the village, Mangrove Bay Road winds around a crescent-shaped bay, which long ago lost its mangroves but is nevertheless a beautiful bay. The Somerset Country Squire, off **Mangrove Bay**, is a pleasant pub for lunch, dinner, or a drink. **Cavello Bay**, a ferry stop on the Great Sound, at the end of Scotts Hill Road, is another stunning sight, and the residential area around it is quite charming. This is a great place to stroll around to see how Bermudians live, away from the tourist attractions.

If you continue straight along Cambridge Road, you'll reach Cambridge Beaches, one of the island's premier cottage colonies, which occupies a 10-hectare (25-acre) peninsula, fringed with five beaches. In addition to its wonderful cottages, Cambridge Beaches has an outstanding two-storey spa. In this area, too, is spectacular ★★★ **Somerset Long Bay**, whose quiet pretty park is fine for picnicking and sandy beach is good for sun worshipping.

Mangrove Bay Road leads to ★ **Watford Bridge**, a long bridge with splendid views that connects Somerset Island with Watford and Boaz Islands. There is another ferry landing here, and at the foot of the bridge, Greg Hartley's Under Sea Adventure (tel: 234-2861) departs aboard the glass-bottom boat, the *Rainbow Runner*. Adventurers wear helmets and descend about 3 metres (10ft) to explore Bermuda's coral reefs. There are changing facilities aboard the boat, so don't forget to bring along a bathing suit and towel.

Across Watford Bridge Somerset Road becomes Malabar Road. (It's the only road that traverses the small islands that lead to the Royal Naval Dockyard, so you can't get lost on it.)

At the other end of Watford Island there is a small cemetery, the ★ **Royal Naval Cemetery**. As the name suggests, the graveyard is the final resting place for seamen and their families who have died in or near Bermuda since the Royal Navy began the operation of this Atlantic station almost two centuries ago. The cemetery is not only an interesting source of unusual information, but also contains some moving poetry. The headstones reveal much about the lives of those buried here; causes of death describe accidents and epidemics of yellow fever, infant mortality, and

drowning. Collectively, the graves offer an unusual insight into the social conditions of that bygone era which did so much to develop the West End.

Fish and ships at the Royal Naval Dockyard

Detour off Malabar Road to the right on Lagoon Road, which goes down into a pretty inlet called The Crawl, picturesque **Lagoon Park**, and a little beach at Parsons Bay. This area, thick with mangroves, is a good place for swimming, bird-watching, and picnicking.

39

Continuing along the stretch of bridge-connected islands you'll come to the Royal Naval Dockyard. Following the American victory in its war for independence from Great Britain, England began to feel the need for a shipyard and fortification in the Atlantic. Preliminary construction began on the ★★★ **Royal Naval Dockyard** in 1809, with the work being done by slave labour and hundreds of convicts who were sent from England for the purpose, and continued until the mid-19th century. The fortress was formidable, huge constructions of stone, with walls 1 metre (3 ft) thick, cover 10 hectares (25 acres) of Ireland Island. The Royal Navy occupied Dockyard (as it's called by all Bermudians) until 1951, and some years passed before it assumed its present role. You don't need a pass or a ticket to enter, you just drive in between two stone pillars that are capped with antique lanterns.

Stroll along Clocktower Centre

On your left as you go in you'll see Freeport Seafood Restaurant, where there are tables both indoors and al fresco, and on your right is Dockyard Watersports, the take-off point for parasailing and boating. The sightseeing trimaran *Hat Trick* and the catamaran *Restless Native* take on passengers here, and there is also a boat-rental place.

Straight ahead is **Clocktower Centre**, an indoor pedestrian mall whose sundry boutiques purvey items such as Havana cigars, Black Seal rum, sunglasses, designer perfumes, basketry and batik crafts, cashmere sweaters,

Cannon protect the Museum

Flags in the Frog & Onion

Distinctive ceramic art

swimsuits, and Haagen Dazs ice cream. Tucked into a corner of the mall is Beethoven's Restaurant, which has moderately priced breakfast, lunch, afternoon tea, and dinner.

On 17 February, 1975, Queen Elizabeth II officially opened the **Maritime Museum** (tel: 234-1418; 9.30am–4.30pm May–November and 10am–4.30pm December–April), which sprawls over 2 hectares (6 acres) beyond the Clocktower Centre. The huge facility, approached on a short drawbridge over a moat, occupies the old keep of the fortress and six former supply storehouses. The old stone buildings now contain extensive exhibits of everything from ancient bottles to Bermuda fitted dinghies. The Age of Discovery exhibit hall was opened in 1992 by Diego Colón, on the 500th anniversary of the year his ancestor famously sailed the ocean blue.

Across the street from the Maritime Museum, the **Cooperage** now houses the Neptune Cinema, which shows first-run feature films; the Frog & Onion Pub restaurant, a great favourite of Bermudians as well as tourists; and the Craft Market (tel: 234-3208; 9.30am–5pm daily), where local crafts are sold, and where you can observe works-in-progress of some artisans in their studios. The miniature cedar furniture made by Jack and Celia Arnell are among the crafts that can be found here, as well as jewellery made by Judith Faram, and the little angels and dolls which Ronnie Chameau creates from dried banana, grapefruit, and palm leaves.

The nearby **Bermuda Arts Centre** (tel: 234-2809, 10am–5pm daily) is a sophisticated gallery that was opened by Princess Margaret in 1984. Among its exhibits are the fascinating photographs of Mark Emmerson, oil paintings by Elmer Midgitt and by Sheilagh Head, beautiful costume dolls made by Kathleen Kemsley Bell, and many other works by local artists, some of whom have studios here. Other studios nearby are Island Pottery (tel: 234-3361; 9.30am–5pm) and Bermuda Clayworks (tel: 234-5116; 9.30am–5pm). Not far away, the Pirate's Landing is a family-style restaurant, and behind the Cooperage there is a beach and snorkel park. Club 21, a popular jazz club open only in high season, is in a small stone building not far from the one that houses Bermuda Clayworks.

Looming high on a bluff is the **Commissioner's House**, reputedly the world's first cast-iron-framed large building. Construction began on the massive structure in 1823, and between 1827 and 1837 this was the home of the commissioner. In addition to its cast-iron trusses and girders, the house has mahogany woodwork, marble fireplaces, and marble baths. In 1919, this building was officially designated the *HMS Malabar*. At press time, it was not open to the public because a $3 million restoration project was in progress.

Route 5

Spittal Pond

Tour of South Road *See map on pages 24–25*

South Road takes you along some of Bermuda's best beaches, with about 23 wonderful pink velvety sands and picturesque coves stretching from Tucker's Town to Southampton. But there are plenty of other attractions in between. This tour begins at Spittal Pond and goes along South Road, which merges with Middle Road in the western part of the island, and ends at Gibb's Hill Lighthouse.

The 25-hectare (60-acre) ★★★ **Spittal Pond**, a showpiece of the National Trust, is the largest and most easily accessible of the island's nature reserves. It's a vast open space, lush with vegetation, where during the year more than two dozen migratory birds hang out. It's also a great place for hiking enthusiasts – trails lace around the brackish pond, and visitors are admonished not to stray off the marked pathways.

At the south end, along the ocean, a bronze plaque marks the place where some of the early settlers found what came to be called **Spanish Rock**. The rock they chanced upon had some crude carvings engraved on it, including numbers that are believed to be the date 1543. In modern times, historians researching the conundrum are convinced that the lettering and numbers were made by sailors from a Portuguese ship that came ashore here in the year 1543.

Around 1900 a lead cast was made of the carvings – which have long since been obliterated – and in 1940 the bronze plaque was made from the cast at Royal Naval Dockyard. A plaster-of-Paris mould of the 16th-century rock markings can be seen in Hamilton, at the Museum of the Bermuda Historical Society.

41

Sunday best

In this vicinity is **Jeffrey's Hole**, so-called because – according to local lore – an escaped slave hid here. And nearby, at the western end of the nature reserve, is the **Checkerboard**, an area where the limestone appears to have been cut into chessboard-like squares.

Heading westwards along South Road you'll come shortly to Collector's Hill, where there is a little shopping centre with a pharmacy and the **Speciality Inn**, a small restaurant, popular with locals, that serves pizza and sandwiches.

Collector's Hill came by its name in the early 19th century, when a customs collector had a home near its summit. Drive up the steep hill to view ★★★ **Verdmont** (tel: 236-7369; 10am–4pm, closed Sunday and Monday), a lovely house museum surrounded by a walled garden. Built in about 1710 by a prominent ship-owner by the name of John Dickinson and reminiscent of an English country estate, the four-squared house was designed in the transitional style, with both 17th-century medieval and 18th-century Georgian architectural elements. There are two chimneys at each end of the house, and a fireplace in each of the eight rooms. The sash windows, 12 x 12, are believed to be original to the house. The balcony on the front was added by the Bermuda National Trust, which now owns and maintains Verdmont, as were the restored beams and rafters. Two large downstairs rooms were a parlour and drawing room, with connecting double doors that could be opened to accommodate large gatherings.

The panelling of Georgia pine was an 18th-century addition, as were the shutters and cornices. The collection of cedar furnishings, though not original to the house, is perhaps the best on the island; much of it was made by Bermuda cabinetmakers between 1700 and 1820. A cedar desk in the drawing room, its lid and sides made of single

Verdmont

Treasures inside Verdmont

planks, dates from about 1780, and a cedar corner cabinet in the parlour also dates from the late 18th century. Some of the fireplace mouldings are cedar, said to be as old as the house.

While the furnishings are not original to Verdmont, some of the portraits were painted in the house between 1765 and 1775. There are good collections of 17th- to 18th-century china and porcelain; a French blue-and-gold coffee service was captured by a Bermudian privateer in 1815. The nursery, with its period furnishings and children's objects, is charming. And in the attic you can see how traditional Bermuda roofs are constructed.

Ariel statue stands guard

To your left on South Road you will see the entrance to ★★**Palm Grove** (9am–5pm, closed Friday through Sunday). This is a handsome house although it's not open to the public. However, visitors are welcome to enter the grounds to see the large pond, wherein there is a relief map of Bermuda, with the parishes clearly indicated. The 7-hectare (18-acre) estate is beautifully landscaped, and decorated with a moon gate and Desmond Fountain statues.

43

From Palm Grove turn left on the main road, and you'll very shortly see the entrance (on your left) to **Ariel Sands**, a cottage colony associated with the film actor Michael Douglas, whose mother is Bermudian. This property is owned by her family, but in 1997 Douglas took a more active role, spending a good chunk of money getting it all spiffed up. The Ariel Sands beach is beautiful, with two ocean-fed pools – a graceful statue of Ariel balances out in the ocean – and Caliban's is an excellent restaurant for lunch or dinner, and very popular with Bermudians.

The next sight on this route is the ★★★**Botanical Gardens** (tel: 236-4201; open sunrise to sunset daily), which is a wonderful showcase for Bermuda flora. Under the auspices of the Agricultural Department and established around the turn of the 20th-century, the 15-hectare (36-acre) gardens are awash with beautiful indigenous shrubs, flowering plants, and trees, which are labelled. Included in the acreage is an orchard, a miniature jungle, and a sweetly scented garden for the blind. At the visitors centre you can pick up lots of friendly information and a map, and watch a short introductory video. And there's also a little gift shop where you can buy souvenirs and snacks. Seventy-five-minute guided tours are conducted at 10.30am, Tuesday, Wednesday, and Friday.

An old Indian Laurel tree

Camden, the residence of Bermuda's premier, is also on the grounds of the Botanical Gardens. A beautiful 3-storey white house with graceful verandas, Camden, which was built in the 1700s, is open for tours on Tuesday and Friday from noon until 2pm, except when official functions are scheduled. Admission is free.

Floral carpet at Camden

From the Botanical Gardens, turn right and go west on South Road. This is Paget Parish, where there are slews of hotels, guest houses, and apartments. And beaches. Just past Stowe Hill Road you'll come to Rural Hill, where there is a small shopping plaza. The **Ice Queen** is a good place to stop for a refreshing ice cream. Although it's only a take-out place, the Ice Queen is a popular after-hours spot, where youthful Bermudians gather after the nightclubs close for burgers, and the plaza is jammed with cars till the small hours.

Grape Bay Drive, which feeds into Rural Hill, is a long beautiful street that leads to Grape Bay Cottages which sit just above a very pretty beach nestled among bay grape trees. The area is ideal for beach lovers and honeymooners. Beyond Grape Bay Drive, White Sands Drive also leads to a lovely beach, with public access next to the entrance to the White Sands Hotel, which stands on a cliff overlooking the beach. At the end of White Sands Road an unpaved right-of-way meanders through an overhanging growth of oleanders and bay grape trees directly onto the beach itself. There are no public facilities, and limited shade, so it's not a place where anybody should spend too much time in the heat of the day, but the location is spectacular and a perfect setting for an early morning swim. Having seen for yourself how lovely it is, you might like to return in the evening for a moonlight dip.

Elbow Bay, Paget
Ritzy cottages

A little after Rural Hill Plaza is the **Paget Marsh Nature Reserve**, a 7-hectare (18-acre) place where endangered trees and shrubs grow. The nature reserve is administered by the Bermuda National Trust (tel: 236-6483), and an appointment must be made to wander through it.

South Road merges with Middle Road, with South Road going off to your left. Rounding the curve you'll see in front of you the Harmony Club, Bermuda's only all-inclusive couples-only hotel. Continuing around on South Road you'll pass Loughlands, a handsome white Bermuda mansion that is now a moderately-priced guest house, and Skytop Cottages, tourist apartments atop a hillside surrounded by a citrus grove. On the left you'll see the entrances to the Stonington Beach Hotel and the Elbow Beach Resort, both of which sit above marvellous beaches. For a small fee non-guests may use the Elbow Beach facilities, which include changing rooms and a snack bar. Stonington Beach Hotel is the training ground for students of the Bermuda Hospitality and Culinary Institute.

South Road veers off to the left, and just in front of you is the entrance to the ritzy Horizons & Cottages, a very showy Relais & Châteaux property. There is also the posh members-only Coral Beach Club, which occupies a splendid stretch of pink sand just south of the hotel.

Along this stretch of the road you'll drive by two lush beachside parks, ★★★ **Astwood Park** and ★★★ **Warwick Long Bay**. These beaches are splendid, but they are public – no admission is charged – and therefore crowded in the summer. There are picnic tables and toilet facilities, but no lifeguards. Across the road from Astwood Park are the Astwood Cove guest houses, while just to the east are the Marley Beach Cottages, which perch high on a cliff overlooking another great beach. The scenery is so spectacular that scenes for the film *The Deep* were shot here.

At Warwick Long Bay, South Road is high above the cliffs and the beach is accessible via a picturesque winding pathway which descends through sand-dunes. The partially-solidified dunes are dotted with a variety of flowering bushes and the distinctive, spiky century plants, members of the lily family, which are also known as American aloes.

From Warwick Long Bay, you can walk all the way to Chaplin Bay and on to Horseshoe Bay, Jobson Cove and so on. In total, the sandy beaches extend along this part of the shore almost without interruption for about a mile. The walk can be made even longer, and is particularly delightful, if you choose to walk along the beaches and then return following the well-defined pathways that meander among the sand-dunes.

In the vicinity of **Horseshoe Bay** – which must surely be Bermuda's most photographed beach – there are several cliffs adjacent to the beach and at the water's edge; climbing to the top of their peaks can afford some breathtaking views of the reefs, and colour patterns out to sea. Between February and August, hundreds of longtails make their nests in these cliffs and provide a spectacular sight for birdwatchers. At Horseshoe Bay there is a snack bar and such luxuries as a foot shower and changing facilities.

Rugged Warwick Long Bay

Jobson Cove

45

Sundown at Horseshoe Bay

Gibbs Hill Lighthouse

Crossing into Southampton Parish, you'll see on your right the Southampton Princess Hotel, one of Bermuda's largest hotels, which stands high up on a hill. This hotel is the sister of the Hamilton Princess in the capital. Past the Southampton Princess golf course and the Henry VIII pub on your right you'll come to ★★★ **Gibbs Hill Lighthouse** (tel: 238-0524; 9am–4.30pm). The lighthouse is 35 metres (117ft) tall, and stands on a hill 72 metres (239ft) high, all of which makes for truly spectacular views. Despite its age – it opened in 1846 – the light can be seen by ships 64 km (40 miles) out to sea, and by planes 190 km (120 miles) away at 3,000 metres (10,000ft). One hundred and eighty-five steps spiral up to the top, with platforms where you can rest and historical displays you can examine along the way. Incidentally, the tower does sway in a high wind, and Bermuda has plenty of very high winds. In the old lighthouse keeper's cottage, the delightful Lighthouse Tearoom (tel: 238-8679) is open for breakfast, lunch, and afternoon tea, when crumpets and scones are served: a most pleasant place.

Across South Road from the Lighthouse, down a winding entrance road, lies the Sonesta Beach Resort & Spa. A big splashy resort, the **Sonesta** is the only hotel in Bermuda that has rooms from which you can step directly onto a sandy beach. The hotel has three beaches, in a dramatic setting of craggy cliffs. Nearby is the Reefs, a small very stylish hotel in a likewise scenic setting. One of the Reefs' restaurants, Coconuts, is down close to the water.

The charming Royal Heights Guesthouse is very close to the Lighthouse. And south shore beaches are not far away: **Church Bay**, a good snorkelling beach, and its pretty park lie on the shore just before South Road merges with Middle Road. From here you can continue to explore the west of the island (*see Routes 3 and 4*), or return to Hamilton via Middle Road.

Church Bay for snorkellers

Route 6

Tour of Harrington Sound *See map on page 48*

This tour begins at Devil's Hole Aquarium, loops around Harrington Sound – a large saltwater bay in Hamilton almost surrounded by land – and takes in Bailey's Bay.

Fish-friendly angling

The tour begins at the ★ **Devil's Hole Aquarium** (tel: 293-2072; 9.30am–4.30pm, closed in winter). The name is quite a misnomer, so don't expect to see the kind of aquarium you're accustomed to. This is one of Bermuda's oldest and most highly-publicised attractions. Local lore has it that as far back as 1830 a man named Trott charged a fee for people to look at his fish pond here, and promotional materials do date back to 1843. It may be that Trott shrewdly erected a wall around his pond in a deliberate effort to create an aura of mystery and thus interest in it. It's actually a collapsed cave which has a small underwater outlet onto the South Shore. This crack through the rocks facilitates a natural and constant inflow of sea water and enables the regular stock of fish to live quite happily without any need for an artificial water circulating system. It is more like a grotto, or a water hole, teeming with a few hundred apparently ravenous sea creatures.

Upon coughing up the entrance fee visitors are provided with hookless fishing lines and bait, and whatever you catch you toss back in. Devil's Hole derives its name from the loud noise sometimes generated by an inward surge of sea water, and has nothing to do with evil spirits. The sandwich shop here is even called Angels Wings.

An incidental anecdote about Devil's Hole: it is said that the 1940s international swimming sensation and Hollywood movie star Esther Williams was visiting this spot when she accidentally dropped her purse in among the sharks and turtles. Quite undaunted she casually dived in and retrieved her valuables. This is not recommended to anyone else, however.

Quite near Devil's Hole Aquarium, sitting right on Harrington Sound, is Angel's Grotto, a charming collection of (as Bermudians say) 'self-catering apartments'. Back in the 1930s, this was a popular night club, but for many years it has been a guest house.

This western section is the only part of Harrington Sound Road that affords a view of the water. For most of the way the Sound is hidden from view by houses, shrubs, and trees; along much of it you have very little sense that you're actually circling the water. Nevertheless, it's a very pretty drive, with lots of lush vegetation.

Palm shaded church on the Sound

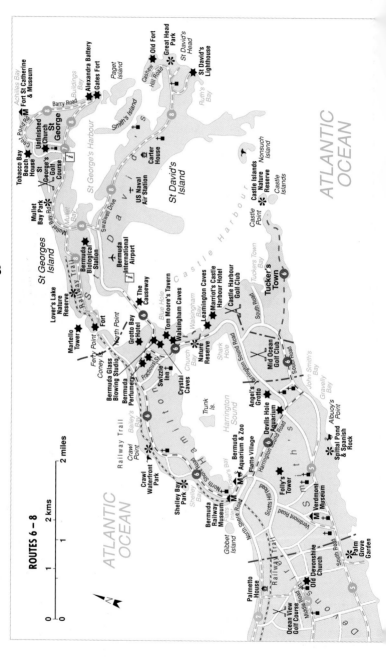

ROUTES 6 – 8

ATLANTIC OCEAN

ATLANTIC OCEAN

N

0   1   2 miles
0   1   2 kms

St Georges Island

St David's Island

St George's Harbour

Castle Harbour

Harrington Sound

Smith's

Fort St Catherine & Museum
Achilles Bay
Coot Pond
Buildings
Unfinished Church
St George
Barry Road
St George's Golf Course
Tobacco Bay Beach House
Mullet Bay Park
Mullet Bay
Bay Road
Lover's Lake Nature Reserve
Bermuda Biological Station
Railway Trail
Martello Tower
Ferry Point
Coney I.
North Point
Fort
Bermuda Glass Blowing Studio
Bermuda Perfumery
Crystal Caves
Grotto Bay Hotel
Swizzle Inn
Flatts Rd.
Tom Moore's Tavern
The Causeway
Walsingham Caves
Blue Hole
Nature Reserve
Leamington Caves
Marriott's Castle Harbour Hotel
Castle Harbour Golf Club
Walsingham
Bay
Church
Bay
Shark
Hole
Alexandra Battery
Gates Fort
Castle Hill Road
Old Fort
Great Head Park
St David's Head
St David's Lighthouse
Paget Island
Ruth's Bay
Carter House
US Naval Air Station
Castle Islands Nature Reserve
Nonsuch Island
Castle Islands
Castle Point
Tucker's Town
Tucker's Town Bay
South Road
Mid Ocean Golf Club
South Road
John Smith's Bay
Gravelly Bay
Albuoy's Point
Angel's Grotto
Devils Hole
Aquarium
Spittal Pond & Spanish Rock
Bermuda Aquarium & Zoo
Flatts Village
Folly's Tower
Verdmont Museum
Verdmont Road
Harrington Sound Road
Harrington Sound Road
North Shore Road
Crawl Waterfront Park
Shelley Bay Park
Bermuda Railway Museum
Shelley Bay
Railway Trail
Crawl Point
Bailey's Bay
Flatts Inlet
Trunk Is.
Bermuda International Airport
Swainnell Drive
Mullet Bay
Scotts Hill Rd.
Palmetto House
Ocean View Golf Course
Middle Road
Old Devonshire Church
Palm Grove Garden
South Road
North Shore Road
Railway Trail
Gibbet Island
6
7
8
8
8
6
6
6
6
6
5
5
5
2
1
7
i
i

To the south of here there is a public beach and good snorkelling at John Smith's Bay, and further east off South Road is the Pink Beach Club, one of the island's cottage colonies. A bit further east still, on the south shore, Tucker's Town is a posh residential community, with the members-only Mid-Ocean Club and Golf Course and multi-million-dollar estates. Tucker's Town is named after the early 17th-century governor Daniel Tucker, who wanted to move the capital to this spot. Of course, that never happened.

If you're of an athletic bent, you may want to go east on South Road, south of the Mid-Ocean Club and Tucker's Town Bay, and follow the signs that point to **Castle Harbour Beach** and the Natural Arches. Carved by the wind and water, the limestone rocks form arches that rise up 10 metres (35ft) above the beach.

Members only at Mid-Ocean Club
The Natural Arches

This long narrow peninsula juts out into **Castle Harbour**, and off its tip, across a narrow strait, is **Castle Island**. There is a protected nature reserve on the island, and the remains of a 17th-century fort. This was one of the first forts erected, and legend has it that a Spanish galleon was frightened off with the firing of one cannonball from the Castle Island guns. The galleon retreated, not knowing that the fort had used up exactly one-third of its supply: there were only two cannonballs remaining in the fort's arsenal. Beyond Castle Island, across the harbour, strangely named **Nonsuch Island** is a restricted bird sanctuary which is a site for studying endangered species.

Follow Harrington Sound Road along the western shore of the Sound. Harrington Sound Road, North Shore Road, and Middle Road all converge in **Flatts Village**, a small but utterly charming settlement. The very modestly-priced Brightside Apartments are sited here, right across from the Palmetto Hotel, a lovely hotel with a good restaurant called the Inlet and a pub-like bar. The restaurant is named after **Flatts Inlet**, which winds inland from the sea and then races its way beneath the narrow Flatts Bridge into the calmer waters of Harrington Sound. Shops are scattered along the sides of the inlet, and houses are perched along the adjacent hillsides. A magnificent row of palm trees rises from the waterfront and fish swim among the eddies and changing currents of its sparkling waters.

Fishing in Flatts Village

In days gone by, Flatts was a smugglers' cove, and it is certainly in a good position for clandestine operations. As a matter of fact, it was partly because of smuggling in this area that the capital came to be moved from St George's to Hamilton. Former residents of this area – seafarers by trade – would bring goods directly home, rather than register them at Customs in St George's, which was at that time the capital. It was felt that the capital, with its Customs Office and other administrative office, should be more centrally located than St George's at the far eastern end of the island. The capital was moved to Hamilton in 1815.

A Rock Sound exhibit

Cross Flatts Bridge to reach the ★★★ **Bermuda Aquarium, Natural History Museum & Zoo** (Flatts Village, tel: 293-2727; 9am–5pm, with last admission at 4.30pm) which sits on a promontory in a position which conveniently allows it access to the waters of Harrington Sound. Established in 1926, the aquarium was until fairly recently called the 'Government Aquarium', and funded by public administration. It strives to be self-supporting, through the entrance fee, items sold in the gift shop, and the efforts of 'friends' groups. Among them is the Zoological Society, which brings members together for a variety of interesting workshops and fund-raising projects. The zoo complex also houses a small reference library and facilities for on-site research.

The first section houses the aquarium, where all of the fish and marine life indigenous to Bermuda's waters are displayed in tanks. Most of the creatures are acquired by the aquarium staff, though divers and fisherfolk occasionally add to the stock.

Just inside the entrance, pick up an 'electronic wand' for a self-guided tour. Hold the wand in front of an exhibit, and it activates a recorded commentary. You don't have to be a rocket scientist, but if you prefer you can waive the wand and just read the plaques beside each display.

The displays seek to recreate, as far as possible, the actual environment in which each species would normally be found, and to make the visit informative as well as fun. Groupings are also in accordance with natural communities, in which each element is dependent upon and

Children love the North Rock tank

compatible with the other. So for example, moray eels glide and squirm among gnarled and pitted rocks; wrasses, urchins, and squirrel fish inhabit a rocky ledge near a sandy bottom. Particularly noteworthy are the tanks which enable you to have a closer look at turtles, lobsters, and the elegant angelfish. There are miniature tanks which highlight sea life among the inshore mangrove roots, seahorses, and the nocturnal phosphorescence among corals and smaller life forms.

If you've ever wanted to get up-close and almost personal with a shark, this is the place to do it. They swim by at shoulder height, displaying an awesome array of sharp teeth. Kids seem to delight in getting a close-up view of sharks devouring smaller fish.

The aquarium's glamorous showpiece is the $5.2 million, 145,000-gallon North Rock exhibit, unveiled in 1996. It displays a whole variety of reef inhabitants, shark, barracuda, and other sea creatures.

The **Natural History Museum**, in the same building as the aquarium, has displays that explain the volcanic origins of Bermuda, as well as features on scuba diving in the surrounding waters. When you leave this building, you'll pass a pool which is home to a small family of happily frolicking and flapping harbour seals, always great fun to watch at feeding time. Next to it, a lily pond accommodates dozens of Japanese *koi*.

51

Successfully bred in captivity

Don't leave before roaming around the small **zoo**, where there is a collection of alligators, monitor lizards, raccoons, peacocks, a plethora of parrots and a variety of mandarin and mallard ducks. Lizards dart around a nearby enclosure; be sure to take time to see the skink – Bermuda's indigenous member of the lizard family. The skink was the first creature to be seen by the ship-wrecked survivors of the *Sea Venture* in 1609. There is also an Australasian area that's now home to animals from New Guinea, Borneo, and Malaysia.

Of particular interest are the flamingos and Galapagos tortoises, which have been bred successfully in captivity here, and sometimes exported to facilities elsewhere in the world. This experimental, protectionist, and conservationist aspect of the staff's work has earned worldwide respect and resulted in Bermuda's participation in all manner of international projects.

Leaving the aquarium, head north along North Shore Road. The small island you see across the entrance to Flatts Inlet is **Gibbett Island**. In gory days of yore, Gibbett Island is the place where witches were hanged, their bodies left twisting in the wind for all to see. You can also see the bridge pylons for the old Bermuda Railway (*see pages 68–9*), which once crossed the inlet here.

Railroad memorabilia

Presently you will arrive at the ★★ **Railway Museum** and **Curiosity Shop** (37 North Shore Road, tel: 293-1774, 10am–4pm, closed Sunday). Appropriately enough, the museum is housed in the old Aquarium Station of the railroad. It's filled with wonderful memorabilia about 'Old Rattle and Shake'. Footage of the railway in action can be seen, along with marvellous photographs, old signs, and even some wicker chairs from the first-class compartment. Seeing all of it you'll understand why many Bermudians of a certain age are so nostalgic about the train.

Stay on North Shore Road and keep going around the Sound. Shipbuilding was a major activity in this part of the island in earlier times. Bermudians have traditionally been sailors and shipbuilders. Necessity being the mother of invention, they have been so engaged largely because of the island's isolation. In the 19th century, Bermudians sailed down to the Turks and Caicos Islands where they mined salt and sold it in Newfoundland and in the US.

Shelly Bay, now on your left, has the distinction of being the only really good beach on the North Shore. It is a splendid seashore, and a favourite for families: the waters are shallow, and there's a playground. With high north winds, it's a wonderful place for windsurfing. There are public restrooms here, and in the high season, a snack bar and snorkelling equipment rentals. Shelly Bay Park, fringed with mangroves, has shaded tables for picnickers.

When you leave the park and continue east, you'll be travelling up Crawl Hill, at the top of which is another waterside park. There are great views from this park, all along the north coast. During the War of 1812, the great view was not lost on the British. In 1814, Bermuda was the springboard for the British attack on Washington, DC, and it was from the vantage point of a hilltop house veranda in this vicinity that Admiral Sir Alexander Cochrane observed the mustering of the fleet prior to the launch.

Notice on your right Fractious Street – yet another of Bermuda's oddly-named streets. The story behind this one is that the street was named for the horse that belonged to the contractor who built this road.

North Shore Road sweeps southwards and intersects Wilkinson Avenue and Blue Hole Hill Road. The area around the intersection is Bailey's Bay, which is not a watery cove, but a pleasant little residential community. Shortly before the intersection you'll see the ★★ **Bermuda Perfumery** (tel: 293-0627; 9.15am–5pm Monday–Saturday, 10am–4pm Sunday), where fragrances are extracted from local flowers. The perfumery, a family business begun in 1929, is in a 300-year-old farmhouse, and sits on

Scent of Bermuda

2 hectares (6 acres) of land. There are nature trails through the fragrant garden, which is a very relaxing and pleasant place. The factory creates essences of jasmine, frangipani, oleander, and other fragrances, all of which, of course, are for sale in the gift shop.

From the perfumery and garden, cross the intersection and go the short distance on Blue Hole Hill Road to reach the ★★ **Bermuda Glassblowing Studio** (tel: 293-2234; 9am–6pm Monday–Friday and 10am–6pm Saturday–Sunday; 9am–5pm November–April) which will be on your right. A cooperative of eight artisans, the Glassblowing Studio contains a workshop and showroom in which some exquisite glassworks are created and sold. There are demonstrations of the art of glassblowing daily between 9am and 5pm. This may be the hottest spot in all of Bermuda – temperatures reach well over 43°C (110°F) in the work area, and if you take a look into the constantly open furnaces you will feel even hotter.

Glasswork requires skill

There are three furnaces, each of which plays a key role in the manufacturing process. Because hot liquid glass requires an expert hand, the processes involved in melting, blowing, shaping, and detaching the finished article demand skilful dexterity. The artists and their apprentices work together in complete harmony, and the work is done speedily and deliberately – sometimes just a short puff and a whirl before the glass is again plunged back into the glowing inferno of the furnace. This is Bermuda's first and only glassblowing studio. All items have been designed and created on the premises by the artisans you see working. Their work includes bowls, vases, sculptures, and a full range of collectables.

53

You will already have passed the ★★★ **Swizzle Inn**, and perhaps you have enjoyed a well-known drink called a Dark 'n' Stormy. This roadside tavern is immensely

Drinks at the Swizzle Inn

Along the Causeway

View over Castle Harbour

popular for its pub fare and ambience. And of course, for those Dark 'n' Stormies. If you're in the mood for something light, Bailey's Bay Ice Cream Shoppe is just across the street, and they also serve a range of sandwiches.

At this point, you have the option of crossing the Causeway to St David's and St George's islands (*see Route 8*), or continuing around Harrington Sound to investigate some of Bermuda's vast caves and other sights on the eastern shore of the Sound.

If you opt to cross the ★★★ **Causeway** – simply turn right after you leave the Bermuda Glassblowing Studio and continue along Blue Hole Hill Road. Crossing Castle Harbour, Bermuda's second great sound, this impressive 1-km (⅝-mile) structure is certainly well worth seeing. It opened in 1901, replacing an 1871 bridge that was blown away by a hurricane in 1899. As you cross, you will notice over to the left the **Grotto Bay Hotel**, whose cottages cascade down the grassy hill to the waters of Ferry Reach. Beneath the grounds of the Grotto Bay property are two illuminated caves, Cathedral Cave and Prospero's Cave. This hotel is also home to a branch of South Side Scuba and other water sports facilities. Looking southwards from the Causeway, you can see **Marriott's Castle Harbour Hotel**. From the air as you fly into Kindley Field, this terraced hotel is reminiscent of giant white steps leading down the hill to Castle Harbour.

Across the water, the Causeway connects with Longbird Bridge and then merges with Kindley Field Road to join Route 8 where Mullet Bay Road pours across Ferry Reach at the swing bridge (*see page 64*).

If you opt for the caves, turn left off Blue Hole Hill Road after leaving the Glassblowing Studio and turn left again on Wilkinson Avenue. Crystal Caves Road will shortly appear on your left. ★★★ **Crystal Caves** (tel: 293-0640; 9.30am–4.30pm; hours are erratic from November till March), 35 metres (120ft) underground, were discovered quite by accident. In 1907, a couple of boys out playing went in search of an errant ball, and found themselves in a vast and eerie cave. It is not recorded whether or not the boys retrieved the ball. On the tour through the caves, the guide manipulates the lights to show off the silhouettes of the elaborate formations.

Continue circling the Sound and turn onto Leamington Lane to see ★★ **Leamington Caves** (tel: 293-1188; 10am–4pm, closed Sunday). Guided tours take in the amber-hued caves, where the stalagmites and stalactites have created fascinating formations. The caves are on the grounds of the Plantation Restaurant, one of the island's

Crystal Cave

excellent and typically Bermudian eateries. Entry to the caves is free if you spend $10 or more for your meal, which you surely will.

There are more than 110 named caves in Bermuda, a good number of them in this vicinity, but only Crystal and Leamington Caves are open to the public. Crystal Cave is well-illuminated, and the entrances of both caves are not fully excavated. But if you're a seasoned cave enthusiast, call the Bermuda Department of Tourism (tel: 292-0023) to get information about going underground.

A short distance from Leamington Caves, make a turning onto Walsingham Lane, a narrow roadway flanked by a hedgerow of Surinam cherries. Part of the way down the lane on the left hand side is the **I. W. Hughes, Jr. Nature Reserve**, a natural habitat for plants and wildlife which is under the care of the Bermuda National Trust.

Walsingham Lane takes you to **★★ Tom Moore's Tavern**, another popular fine dining restaurant, which sits on Walsingham Bay. The bay is named after a sailor aboard the *Sea Venture*, who is believed to have enjoyed visiting the place. The house itself is named for the Irish poet, but he was not its owner, although he did compose a poem celebrating the calabash tree growing on the property. At the time of Moore's brief stay in Bermuda in 1804, it was the private home of the Trott family, and the poet was a frequent visitor. There is a small mangrove swamp just to the left of the parking area, and if you walk to its edge you can perhaps catch a glimpse of several specimens of mullet swimming idly in the shaded waters among the overhanging vegetation.

Tom Moore's Tavern

At the rear of the main house, there is a tangle of hibiscus and cherry bushes and a jumble of vegetation known as Tom Moore's Jungle.

Waiting on the barber, St George

Storybook view

Route 7

Tour of the Town of St George (also called St George's)
See map on page 57

The colonial history of Bermuda began in 1609, when Admiral Sir George Somers and other survivors of the wrecked *Sea Venture* came ashore on what is now called St George's Island. It was on this island that they built the two ships – the *Deliverance* and the *Patience* – that would take them on to Jamestown, Virginia. Ships arriving later from England docked here, and it was here that the first town was created. The Town of St George (also called locally St George's) was the first capital of Bermuda, and in 1620, Bermuda's first Parliament was instituted here in St Peter's Church. In 1815, the capital was moved to Hamilton, while St George's continued to bask peacefully in the sun.

St George's is a storybook town, with small white-washed or sherbet-coloured buildings, and narrow winding alleys with names that, in days gone by, designated what trades flourished along them – such as Needle and Thread Alley, Printers Alley, and Silk Alley. Broad Alley no doubt denoted its width, and Bridge Street is self-explanatory. It's easy to figure who lived on Old Maid's Lane, and Aunt Peggy's Lane. But what might have inspired the name Shinbone Alley?

The tour begins in **King's Square**, which is vastly different now from what it was in the 17th century when the early settlers arrived. In those days this was merely a marshy inlet, a far cry from the charming square it is today. Stop first at the **Visitors Bureau ❶** (tel: 297-1642, open 9am–4pm Monday–Saturday, 10am–3pm Sunday April–October, and 9.30am–2pm Monday–Saturday,

11am–3pm Sunday November–March) to load up the tote bag with maps and brochures. From there stroll out across a broad footbridge to Ordnance Island for a view of the ★ **Deliverance II ❷**, (tel: 297-1459; 9am–6pm, with reduced hours from November–March), a replica of the 17th-century ship that carried shipwreck survivors to Jamestown, Virginia. A trip below deck is an eye-opener, as you can see how cramped the quarters were for passengers on the voyage. Opposite the ship there is a splendid ★ **bronze statue of Sir George Somers ❸**, sculpted by renowned Bermudian artist Desmond Fountain. The shipwrecking of Somers and his crew not only led to the colonisation of Bermuda, but also, according to some historians, inspired Shakespeare's play *The Tempest* (*see pages 14 and 67*). The small building on Ordnance Island is the cruise ship terminal, where passengers aboard luxury cruise ships calling in St George's go through Customs.

Cross back to King's Square. On Wednesdays during low season, the Department of Tourism conducts walking tours of St George's, hosted by the town crier. Colourfully dressed in 18th-century garb, replete with scarlet tunic,

The Deliverance II

Hard to miss

57

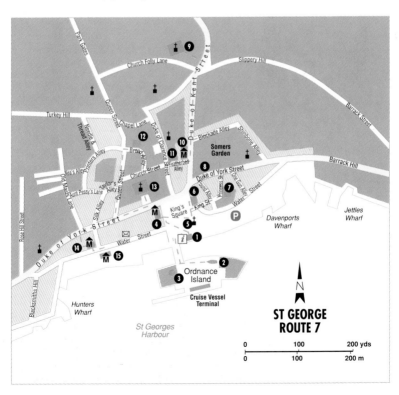

Old-fashioned punishment

breeches, and tricorn hat, the town crier bellows his greetings to the crowd, and then demonstrates some of the punishments that were meted out to wrongdoers in olden days, encouraging visitors to have their pictures taken in the stocks and pillory. Occasionally, costumed actresses show how the nearby **Ducking Stool** was used to punish 'nagging wives and gossips' – by dunking them in the water.

For future reference you may want to note that Freddie's Pub on the square, the White Horse Tavern on the water's edge, and the nearby Carriage House Restaurant are all good lunch options around King's Square.

Opening onto the square, the ★★★ **Bermuda National Trust Museum** ❹ (tel: 297-1423; open 10am–4pm Monday–Saturday, 1–4pm Sunday) is housed in a structure that was built by Bermuda Governor Samuel Day in 1700. For a further 150 years this was the Globe Hotel, and later it became the home of Major Norman Walker, a southerner and Confederate spy during the American Civil War. The Union's blockade of Confederate ports brought on a flurry of blockade-running, with Bermuda – primarily St George's – serving as a transhipment port for southern cotton headed for Europe. 'Rogues and Runners', as the National Trust Museum exhibit is now called, features displays pertaining to that mid-19th century period, with furnishings, documents, ship models, and maps. There is even an antique press that makes souvenir reproductions of the Great Seal of the Confederacy.

Directly across the square from the National Trust Museum, the ★ **Town Hall** ❺ (tel: 297-1532; 10am–4pm, closed Sunday) contains government offices. The ground floor entrance hall is lined with portraits of St George's mayors. In the town hall theatre is a free slide show for visitors, called 'About St George's'. Shows are at 10.05am, 11.05am, and 3.05pm daily except Saturday and Sunday.

Past and present mayors

From the town hall, walk along Bridge Street to see ★★ **Bridge House** ➏ (tel: 297-8211; 9.30am–5.30pm Monday–Saturday, noon–4pm Sunday), a 17th-century two-storey house with double verandas that now contains two private apartments, a crafts shop, and an art gallery. The street and the house were named for a small bridge that in early days crossed a creek in front of the house.

Bridge House

Upon leaving Bridge House, amble up King Street to Princess Street, where the ★★★ **Old State House** ➐ (tel: 292-2480, 297-1206; open 10am–4pm on Wednesday only) sits facing the square. Dating from 1620, this is believed to be the oldest stone building in Bermuda. Before the capital moved to Hamilton, the House of Assembly and the Supreme Court held sessions here. In his book *History of Virginia and the Summers Isles*, published in London in 1624, John Smith described this house as being surrounded by a stockade, with guards in full-dress uniforms guarding the entrance. The guards are long gone, but the building is still quite imposing, if rather small. Nowadays, the State House is leased from the Town of St George by the Lodge of St George No. 200 of the Grand Lodge of Scotland. Each year in April, the solemn Peppercorn Ceremony takes place in King's Square, during which the annual rental fee of one peppercorn is presented by the lodge to the mayor on a velvet pillow.

Old State House

59

Go to your right upon leaving the state house, and walk along Princess Street to ★ **Somers Garden** ➑, a walled area of land with lush plants and tall royal palm trees. There is an obelisk in the garden commemorating the 300th anniversary of the shipwreck of the *Sea Venture*. On a wall nearby, a plaque reads, 'near here was buried the heart of Sir George Somers'. The Admiral quite literally left his heart in Bermuda. Upon completion of the ships, the *Deliverance* and the *Patience*, Somers went on to Jamestown, but he returned to Bermuda and died here in 1610. Before expiring, he asked his nephew, Matthew Somers, to bury his heart here. Matthew is said to have done so, and then secretly stowed his uncle's body on a ship bound for England. Had the body been discovered it would no doubt have been cast overboard, as sailors harboured a great superstition about corpses on ships. But Somers' body survived the voyage and was buried in his native Dorset. On his good-will tour in 1920, on the occasion of the island's Tercentenary, the Prince of Wales broke a bottle of champagne in the park and officially christened it Somers Garden.

Royal palms in Somers Garden

If you go through the park and up the steps to Blockade Alley and turn right on Duke of Kent Street, heading north, you'll arrive at the magnificent ruins of the ★★ **Unfinished Church** ➒, which stands on a hill. The ruins are

Still unfinished

not a result of fire but of neglect. This church, begun in 1874, was meant to replace St Peter's Church, but construction work was abandoned following a schism in the Anglican congregation. The story is told that during excavations for the church, a skeleton was found. Dressed in a French uniform, this was believed to have been the remains of a soldier who was killed during the Gunpowder Plot of 1775 (*see also page 62*). The plot involved a group of Bermudians who were determined to respond to General George Washington, and wrote a letter offering Bermuda's help during the American Revolutionary War. They broke into the powder magazine, and while they were engaged in the theft lookouts were posted to warn them if anyone came along. It is believed that the unfortunate French soldier was simply in the wrong place at the wrong time, and was shot by the lookouts. Now a property of the Bermuda National Trust, which has stabilised and only partially repaired it, the Unfinished Church interior is not open to the public. The ruins are situated on Church Folly Lane, no doubt named for the circumstances that led to the church's abandonment.

Backtrack on Duke of Kent Street to find yourself in the back streets of St George's. Here, it's so easy to imagine the island as it was in its earliest days. There is a charming innocence and serenity in these little winding alleys and narrow passageways, where neighbours chat over fences or tend their gardens. The pale green leaves of banana trees thrust through garden fences, and low white-painted walls are decorated with nasturtiums and wild geraniums.

On Featherbed Alley visit the ★★ **St George's Historical Society Museum** ❿ (tel: 297-0423; 10am–4pm, closed Saturday and Sunday). A private home when it was built in the early 1700s, the house is furnished much as

Banana trees provide shade

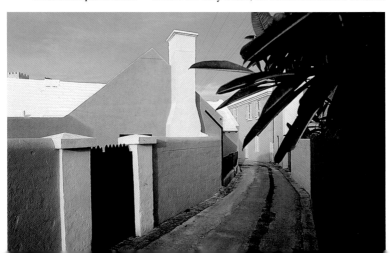

it was then, and contains a wealth of memorabilia and artefacts pertaining to the town's early days. Tucked in the
basement of this house, but with a separate entrance, is the
★★ **Featherbed Alley Printery** ⓫, a tour of which is
included with that of the museum. It houses a working
replica of the Gutenberg Press as well as early editions
of the *Bermuda Gazette*. Joseph Stockdale, who brought
his printing implements from England when he came here,
began publishing the newspaper in 1784, and publication continued without interruption until 1816. Stockdale's
daughters carried on the work after their father's death.
His home, needless to say, was on nearby Printer's Alley.

Turn right upon leaving the Printery and follow Featherbed Alley, crossing Duke of Clarence Street to reach
Church Alley. A few steps along the alleyway you'll come
to Broad Alley, where you can see the ★ **Old Rectory** ⓬
(tel: 297-0878; noon–5pm Wednesday only, November–March only). The charming little one-storey white cottage, which dates to around the turn of the 18th century,
was the early home of the pastor of St Peter's Church.

Chatting at the Old Rectory

Broad Alley winds around and intersects with a tiny
lane called Nea's Alley, which dead-ends at Old Maid's
Lane – and therein lies a tale. The Irish poet, Tom Moore,
spent about four months in Bermuda in 1804, working
as a registrar of courts. During that time he lived in Old
Maid's Lane, where his neighbours were the Richard
Tucker family. Moore wrote soulful odes to 'Nea', and
local lore has it that the object of his affections, his Nea,
was actually Hester, Richard Tucker's wife. No one today
is exactly gossiping in the streets about it, but at the time
their affair seems to have caused quite a stir.

Now make for Duke of York Street via Queen Street
and turn left to arrive at ★★★ **St Peter's Church** ⓭,
which is open daily and for Sunday services. St Peter's
is one of the oldest Anglican churches in the Western
Hemisphere. It is the second church to stand on this site,
the first having been a wooden thatch-roofed structure built
in 1612. Completed in 1619, the present church was se-
verely damaged by a hurricane, and over the years has been
enlarged and altered several times. But this is the same
church in which the Bermuda Parliament was founded
in 1620 – the second oldest Parliament in the world, after England's. The lovely church, with its exposed cedar
beams and handsome brass chandeliers, contains many
treasures, including a 1594 bible; an engraved silver chal-
ice that was presented to the church by the Bermuda Company in 1625, and a communion service that was a gift
from King George III. The cedar altar, dating from 1624,
is said to be the oldest piece of furniture in Bermuda, and
the ironstone font is believed to be from the 15th century.
Among the many memorial plaques on the wall is one

Tucker House

erected to Governor Alured Popple, who died in 1744, at the age of 46. Burial in St Peter's churchyard was discontinued in the mid-19th century, but this is the final resting place for many of Bermuda's early citizenry, and for soldiers and seamen from faraway places.

If you go west on Duke of York Street, you'll arrive at ★★★ **Tucker House ⑭** (tel: 297-0545; 10am–4pm, closed Sunday), another property of the Bermuda National Trust. Exactly when the house was built is not known, but in 1775 it was purchased by Henry Tucker, who was at the time Colonial Treasurer and President of the Governor's Council. The Tucker family has been prominent in Bermudian history since its earliest days. Henry Tucker was a descendant of Daniel Tucker, who came from England in 1616 as Bermuda's second governor. Henry was born in 1742, at the Grove, the Tucker family estate in Southampton parish. Shortly after moving into the house, President Tucker became involved in the locally notorious Gunpowder Plot. His father, Colonel Henry Tucker, was believed to have been among the conspirators who broke into the arsenal and stole gunpowder, which they took to Tobacco Bay, loaded on whale boats, and dispatched to Boston to aid the American Revolutionary Army.

The furnishings in this house, including collections of silver and some fine cedar and mahogany pieces, came from members of the Tucker family. According to local legend, in the mid-19th century, the kitchen was the barber shop of Joseph Hayne Rainey, a free black man from South Carolina who later became the first black man elected to the US House of Representatives. The existence of the barber shop may be in doubt, but the facts about Rainey's political career are correct. He returned to South Carolina after the Civil War, where he served in the state senate before his 1870 election to the Congress

Before leaving the house, you may want to step down to the basement, where **The Book Cellar** has a good selection of books about Bermuda. And finally, in a tiny room off the cellar, there is a small display of 18th-century archaeological artefacts.

Across Water Street is the ★★★ **Carriage Museum ⑮** (tel: 297-1367; 10am–4pm, closed Saturday and Sunday), to see how Bermudians got about prior to the 1946 introduction of the motor car. There is a fine collection of surreys, broughams, and other carriages.

Horse-drawn vehicles on display

Water Street, like so much of Bermuda, looks like something out of a Dickens novel – a narrow street, these days it is lined with shops, many of them branches of Front Street shops. In nearby restored Penno's, Hunter's and Somers' wharves are more shops, along with the studios of some of Bermuda's craftsmen and artisans.

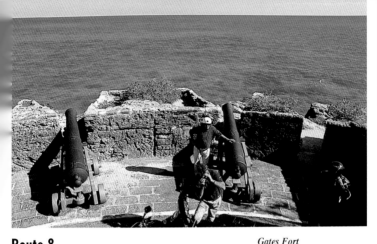

Route 8

Gates Fort

St George's Island and St David's Island *See map on page 48*

This route leaves the Town of St George in two directions, before crossing to St David's Island, which despite the presence of the airport still has plenty to interest.

To see the eastern part of St George's Island, leave town going east on Duke of York Street, which becomes first Barrack Hill Street and then Cut Road. The road swoops south to Gates Bay and ★ **Gates Fort**. The drive along here is quite spectacular. Off to your right in St George's Harbour is Smith's Island, where the English ship, the *Plough*, anchored in 1612, bringing colonists and the first governor, Richard Moore. The bay and the fort are so-named for Thomas Gates, who was the first of the shipwrecked *Sea Venture* survivors to come ashore in July 1609. Gates was on board the ship en route to Virginia to assume his post as Deputy Governor of Jamestown. The present Gates Fort is a reconstruction of a small fort that was erected here in the early 17th century on the orders of Governor Moore.

Taking it easy, St George's

The road leading north from here is Barry Road. A short drive will bring you to the ★ **Alexandra Battery**, a fort built two centuries after Gates Fort. Both forts have free access. The ocean views along here are stunning, but if you're a real fort aficionado, you'll be better served at Fort St Catherine, which we'll visit shortly.

The Alexandra Battery sits adjacent to Buildings Bay. This is where the shipwrecked British built the *Deliverance*, a replica of which you may have seen on Ordnance Island in St George's. Sir George Somers and the other survivors were on the island for nine months after the wreck. Under the supervision of the ship's carpenter,

Fort St Catherine

Richard Frobisher, the *Deliverance* was made using materials salvaged from the *Sea Venture*. Sir George supervised the building of a second ship – the *Patience* – which was made of cedar, and constructed elsewhere on the island.

Continue north on Barry Road to ★★★ **Fort St Catherine** (tel: 297-1920; 10am–4.30pm), which looms above the beach on which the shipwrecked survivors came ashore in 1609. The first Bermudians barely had a toehold on the island before they began constructing this fort. Work on it began in 1613, and continued sporadically until the 19th century, with various enlargements and improvements. Visitors can watch an introductory audio/visual presentation before striking out on a self-guided tour to explore the many tunnels, passageways, and ramparts, perhaps in search of the ghost who is said to hang out here. The exhibits are enlivened by lifelike costumed figures, and there are dioramas to examine, and a display that showcases sparkling replicas of the British crown jewels.

When you leave the fort, go to your right on Coot Pond Road which will take you to ★ **Tobacco Bay**. If you thought to bring your swimming togs, you could now have a dip in the waters off Tobacco Bay. There are changing rooms here, a refreshment stand, and rentals of snorkelling gear. Tobacco Bay played a major role in the Gunpowder Plot of 1775 (*see pages 60 and 62*). This is where the barrels of gunpowder were loaded onto waiting whaleboats, which took them out to two American ships.

Return to the Town of St George on Government Hill Road, which goes by the 18-hole golf course of the St George's Club, a very elegant time-share property. This road becomes Duke of Kent Street and dead-ends at Duke of York Street.

You can take a tour of the rest of St George's Island by going west out of St George's on Duke of York Street, which flows into Duke of Wellington Street and then Mullet Bay Road. Just north of Mullet Bay Park is Tiger Bay Gardens, which was the eastern terminal of the Bermuda Railway, the narrow-gauge railroad that used to run east-west over the island. The Railway Trail (*see pages 68–9*) runs parallel to the main road, going along the northern coast all the way down to Ferry Point Park. The road winds around picture-postcard **Mullet Bay** and continues across the Swing Bridge onto St David's Island (*see opposite*). But for the moment continue straight along Ferry Road.

The southern coast of this peninsula is lush and green, while the windswept northern coast is rocky and barren. As you approach the **Lovers Lake Nature Reserve** you'll be in the vicinity of Vincent Astor's private narrow-gauge railway that connected his Ferry Reach estate with the

Tobacco Bay

Bermuda Railway. The old cemetery in this area is the final resting place for soldiers of the 2nd Battalion, Queen's Royal Rifles, who were buried here in 1864, victims of yellow fever. The soldiers who fell ill that year were quarantined in Ferry Point, but in those days no one knew how the mosquito carried the disease. The men made camp in the worst possible place, in a hollow near a marshland. But at least that year saw the last yellow fever epidemic on the island.

At the end of the peninsula, ★ **Ferry Point Park** is precisely what it says: this was the place where ferries would drop off and pick up passengers. The ferry service was established way back in the earliest days of the colony, when a rowing boat transported passengers across the channel to Coney Island. In those days, though, the ferryman charged for the journey in tobacco.

Coney Island

There are the ruins of several very old forts in Ferry Point Park. The oldest one at the far western point probably dates from the 17th century, while the **Martello Tower** was built in 1823. The fortifications were erected to protect against possible attack through the channel and Ferry Reach.

Backtrack along Ferry Road and turn right along Mullet Bay Road for the swing bridge across Ferry Reach to St David's Island. Before reaching the bridge, you might want to stop off at the ★ **Bermuda Biological Station** (tel: 297-1880, tours Wednesdays at 10am). The Biological Station, or BBSR, an enormous scientific research facility, is among Bermuda's proudest achievements. The idea for this plant began as early as 1896, and in 1903, by agreement with Harvard and New York Universities and the Bermuda Natural History Society, the Biological Station was established. Identified in 1926 by the US National Academy of Sciences as one of three marine laboratories crucial to the health of oceanographic research in the United States, the BBSR was incorporated in New York. Among the research programmes conducted by the station are marine biology and ecology, environmental quality studies, global geosciences, and molecular biology. The Atlantic Global Change Institute, which investigates the societal impacts of global ocean and atmospheric science, is a part of the BBSR.

Martello Tower

The station has a sophisticated high-tech fleet of seven vessels on which research is conducted. There is an annual open house, when visitors are cordially invited to come and learn more about the programmes carried out here, but apart from that and the Wednesday morning tours, it is not open to the public.

At the traffic circle on the other side of the bridge, turn left along Swalwell Drive which then becomes St David's

Cutting-edge marine research

Road. This road skirts the former US Naval Air Station, which was built in 1941 and closed in 1996. The building of the air station was an enormous engineering feat, during which St David's Island and Cooper's Island were re-shaped and merged with some smaller islands to create a larger body of land for the base.

This part of Bermuda figures prominently in the island's earliest history. In 1610, after the death of Sir George Somers and the departure of the *Patience* for England, three men stayed behind. The three rebels – Christopher Carter, Edward Chard, and Robert Waters – were the only humans on the island for two years. During that time, Edward Chard discovered on the beach a large lump of ambergris, which, as a sailor, he knew to be a rare substance discharged by sick whales which was used in the making of perfume. Knowing that what he had found was a treasure, Chard rushed to tell Carter and Waters about it and the three men then hid it away. Naturally, each of the three wanted to reap the full rewards of the find, and not split it three ways.

In 1612, when the *Plough* arrived from England, bringing settlers and the island's first governor – Richard Moore – the three men tried to strike a deal with the ship's captain to privately take the ambergris to England. But for reasons of his own, Christopher Carter decided to tell the new governor of the find, as well as the plot to secrete it on the ship back to England. Chard and Waters were punished, and eventually went on to Jamestown. Carter was offered Cooper's Island as a reward, but – mistakenly thinking there was treasured buried on St David's Island – selected St David's Island instead. His descendants built a stone-and-cedar house here in about 1640, one of the oldest houses on the island.

St David's Island

The air station was literally built around the Carter House, and as long as the station was open, the house was open. Both are now closed, and at press time the future of this historic house was undecided. The Bermuda National Trust (tel: 236-6483) may take it over, which seems a natural progression, given the age of the property and the desire to maintain it. The house contains a treasure of 17th- and 18th-century Bermudian antiques.

Continuing on St David's Road, off to your left in St George's Harbour is Smith's Island, where the *Plough* docked in 1612. The island, and Smith's Parish, were named for Sir Thomas Smith, a major investor in the Bermuda Company.

Presently you'll come to Texas Road, off to your right, which leads out to **St David's Lighthouse**. The lighthouse is open erratically; it's best to call the Park Ranger's Office (tel: 236-5902) to ascertain when it can

Spectacular lighthouse views

be seen. Completed in 1879, the 16-metre (55-ft) lighthouse rises 80 metres (280ft) above sea level. The views from the balcony of the lighthouse are spectacular, of dramatic reefs, small islands, and crashing surf.

St David's Road continues, winding around a bay to Battery Road and **Great Head Park**, Bermuda's easternmost point. Great Head played a part in Bermuda's very early history. After the 1609 shipwreck, eight of the survivors, commanded by Master's Mate Henry Ravens, set out to get help from Virginia in a *Sea Venture* longboat. The boat and passengers disappeared, never to be seen again. But for a two-month period, here on the island, William Strachey lit nightly bonfires to signal to Ravens their location. It was Strachey who later wrote the account of the shipwreck that was allegedly read by William Shakespeare, and perhaps inspired the Bard to write *The Tempest*.

Great Head Park

The fort that can be seen here was built in the late 1800s. The story is told that when King George V died in 1936, the fort was instructed to fire the customary 21-gun salute. The order was issued in the wee small hours of the morning. For some reason no blanks could be found, and after it was ascertained that no ships were due to call, real shots were fired. When the sun came up a Bolivian gunboat sat in the harbour, its crew curious to know why they had been fired upon.

67

If you go straight on the main road instead of turning onto Battery Road, you'll find yourself on the strangely-named Cashew Hill Road. At the very end of the road is **Dennis's Hideaway**, a casual restaurant operated by Dennis Lamb, one of the island's most colourful characters. His speciality is shark hash, but you may not get anything unless you call first to see if he's open (tel: 297-0044).

Shark hash is Dennis's speciality

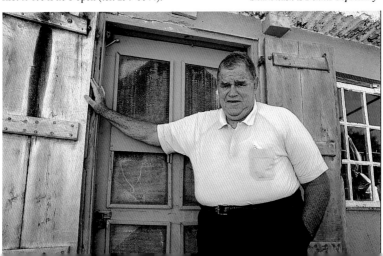

View over Shelly Bay

The Bermuda Railway Trail

This route describes the trail that follows the roadbed of the old narrow-gauge Bermuda Railroad, which operated from 1931 to 1946.

Bermudians old enough to remember when the Bermuda Railway operated from the far east to the far west end usually remember it with great fondness, and many wish that it were still in operation. But the laying of the 34 km (21 miles) of tracks was, as the saying goes, no mean feat. The idea for a railroad seems to have been nurtured as early as 1899, but construction did not actually begin until 1922. The company that was formed to finance the operation had to turn to private speculators in England for the initial capital investment of £100,000.

As construction inched along at the rate of 4 km (2½ miles) a year, the narrow-gauge Bermuda Railroad gained the dubious distinction of being, mile-for-mile, the most expensive railway in history. It took on its first passengers in 1931, after the ceremonious ribbon cutting, and ran from St George's to Somerset. Apparently it was not all smooth riding – islanders nicknamed it 'Old Rattle and Shake.' Passengers in first-class sat in wicker chairs; second-class travellers had to make do with benches. Most of the route ran along the shoreline, but the train did go smack down Front Street in Hamilton.

Walking the Railway Trail

To put it mildly, the railroad was not a money-making enterprise. Investors lost their shirts. The train ceased operating, and in 1946 the Government acquired the Bermuda Railroad for £115,000. Faced with a million-pound repair bill, the Government sold the railway, and in 1948 the whole shooting match – lock, rolling stock, and barrel – was sold and packed off to what was then British Guiana, now Guyana.

But all is not totally lost. The tracks are long gone, but the old railroad bed has another lease on 'life'. In 1984, on the island's 375th anniversary, the Bermuda Government dedicated the land and work began on clearing the overgrown railbed and creating a Railway Trail for hikers, cyclists, horseback riding and motorists. There's even a Railway Museum, a delightful place that occupies the old Aquarium Station in Flatts Village. The Bermuda Department of Tourism publishes a Railway Trail walking guide that describes the sights to be seen along roughly 29 km (18 miles) of trail. While the track was originally 34 km (21 miles) long, the trail is 5 km (3 miles) shy because of the build-up of the roads around Hamilton.

The walking trails can take anything from 1½ to 3 hours to negotiate. You can even plan a walk along the trail and then pick up a bus to take you back to your hotel. Depending on the trail you choose this is an excellent way to see and even stop off and visit some of Bermuda's popular sights, including **South Shore Beach Parklands**, **Gibbs Hill Lighthouse**, **Somerset Bridge and Village**, **Fort Scaur**, **Elys Harbour**, **Palmetto Park**, **Shelly Bay Park and Nature Reserve**, **Harrington Sound** and **Sugarloaf Hill** with its stunning views over St George.

All across the island, Railway Trail signs are posted at each of the access points. Because the trail obviously follows the old railroad track, it goes mostly through the countryside. In some places it's little more than a footpath, where on occasions it's difficult to pick out the trail. And there are some stretches where vehicles are not allowed. There are several places where the trail detours and you must walk along the main roads: these are spots where the original trains faced obstacles such as waterways.

Forced to lay the track as near to the shore as possible in many areas, the railway engineers found themselves having to resort to bridging the river in places, and in fact one-tenth of the entire track was carried on 33 trestle bridges, 16 of which crossed over water. Naturally, swing bridges were required, as well as long tunnels, passing loops, and unstaffed crossings.

Because it is for the most part isolated out in the country, it's very quiet and peaceful. And for those very reasons, you should not take to the trail alone. Bermudians are very friendly, and the crime rate is quite low, but the island has experienced some drug-related problems, and there's no point in going out on a limb and asking for trouble. Needless to say, walking is best done in the morning, before it gets too hot, but in any case wear a hat to shield you from the sun, and comfortable shoes. Parts of the trail are unshaded and quite rugged. Take a camera.

Walking in the morning is best

Crumpets and Calypso

As Great Britain's oldest Crown Colony, Bermuda holds dear many of the traditions of the Mother Country. Parliament is ceremoniously convened, the Queen's Birthday is observed, cricket is virtually the national sport, and tea is served at 4pm. The culture and customs of this island are for the most part very different from Bermuda's cousins in the Caribbean; however, West Indian influences are definitely at play. Reggae and Calypso are very popular here, but the West Indian influence is most obvious in the island's famous Gombey Dancers. The Gombeys are groups of men and boys who perform lively dances that feature shrill whistles, snare drums, and call-and-response rituals. No songs are sung, but the highly stylized movements and sounds narrate stories, often of Biblical events.

"Casanova" entertains

The tradition of the Gombeys, who are black, dates back to the early 19th century, with roots in West Africa. Their costumes and rituals are similar to the Mardi Gras Indians in New Orleans and the Junkanoo performers in the Bahamas. They wear tall pointed hats and brilliantly coloured costumes. In addition to appearances at various times throughout the year, traditionally on Boxing Day (26 December) and New Year's Day, there is an annual Gombey Competition, usually held at one of the major hotels. If you're on the island between November and March, you're guaranteed to see the Gombeys. They perform every Tuesday afternoon at the No. 1 Cruise Shed on Front Street in Hamilton.

71

Theatre

The **Jabulani Repertory Company** presents contemporary plays at the Hamilton Princess Hotel. Combination Dinner/Theatre tickets are sold, or you can opt for only the theatre. Typical productions of the Jabulani include *Driving Miss Daisy* and *The Odd Couple*. The **Daylsford Theatre** mounts a series of plays and theatrical readings. And Bermuda is the only place outside of the US where the famed **Harvard Hasty Pudding Theatricals** are presented, usually in March or April.

Music

The **Bermuda Philharmonic Orchestra** performs in the Bermuda Cathedral, and presents outdoor concerts when weather permits. The Band and Corps of Drums of the **Bermuda Regiment**, along with the **Bermuda Islands Pipe Band and Dancers**, regularly perform the age-old Beating Retreat Ceremony in Hamilton, St George's, and at the Royal Naval Dockyard. And, of course, this being a British Colony, there is a **Gilbert and Sullivan Society**, which presents musicals from time to time.

Regiment Band members

A unique Bermudian moon gate

Architecture

Jalousies provide shade

The island's indigenous architectural style features limestone houses painted in ice-cream and candy colours, each house with a pristine white sloping roof. As is the case in most localities, architects here bow to the demands of nature. Houses made of stone, rather than wood, are better able to withstand the hurricane-force winds that can sweep across the island in the late summer, and the stepped roofs are designed to drain off rainwater into cisterns. Butteries – small outbuildings – also pastel-coloured and with high white stepped roofs, once kept milk and butter cool, and can be seen around the island.

'Welcoming arms' steps are a feature of many Bermuda homes: the banisters curve outwards at the bottom, imitating arms outstretched in greeting. The island is noted for its knee-high fireplaces, which are commonplace in almost all hotel public rooms. Many buildings have ceilings which are shaped like inverted trays.

Hotels must conform to strict standards of architecture. Also pastel-coloured, they have no big signs and no flashing neon. (There are also no billboards on the island; these are strictly forbidden.) Every hotel displays a tasteful plaque that announces its name. Large hotels are not difficult to spot, but it's very easy to cruise by some of the smaller guesthouses: not only are the signs small, but they are often tucked behind a pretty, flowering shrubbery.

Moon gates are another feature unique to Bermuda. These perpendicular limestone archways can be seen in gardens all over the island. **Par-la-Ville Gardens** in Hamilton has moon gates, and so does **Palm Grove** on South Road in Devonshire Parish. It's considered good luck for newlyweds to stand inside one.

Artists and Galleries

The beauty of Bermuda, with its dazzling turquoise waters, pastel-coloured houses, and profusion of subtropical foliage, is a natural inspiration for the artistically inclined. Bermuda has a very lively artist community, with crafts ranging from the stunning life-size bronze figures created by the island's famous sculptor, Desmond Fountain, to miniature cedar furnishings.

Sir George Somers captured by Fountain

The **Bermuda National Gallery** in City Hall, of which Bermudians are justifiably proud, is a climate-controlled facility that exhibits the works of local artists, and also has in its permanent collection works by Rembrandt, Gainsborough, Romney, and Winslow Homer.

City Hall is also home to the permanent collection of the **Bermuda Arts Society**, which exhibits Bermudian artists, as does the **Windjammer Gallery**. The **Masterworks Foundation Gallery** on Front Street has an extensive collection of works by local artists, and some Bermuda inspired pieces by foreign artists. The **Bermuda Arts Centre** and the **Craft Market** at Dockyard feature made-in-Bermuda works by many different artists and craftspeople. The gallery of **Desmond Fountain** is in the Southampton Princess Hotel. Fountain's works include the magnificent statue of Sir George Somers on Ordnance Island in St George's.

73

The acrylic paintings of **Michael Swan** can be found at his galleries at Dockyard and Butterfield Place in Hamilton, and the watercolours of **Carole Holding**, **Joan Forbes**, **Diana Amos**, and **Mary Zuill** can be viewed in galleries all over the capital. The island's most famous watercolourist was the late **Alfred Birdsey**, whose daughter Joanne, a painter herself, maintains his studio. His work can be viewed at galleries on and off the island.

Bermuda has galleries galore

Stephen Card, a former captain in the British Merchant Marines, specialises in marine art, and his works are exhibited at Heritage House in Hamilton. Local architecture is the subject of oil paintings by **Sheilagh Head**, **Elmer Midgett**, and **Bruce Stuart**, and seascapes are captured by **John Kaufman**. Photographers whose work focuses on local scenes include **Mark Emmerson**, **Judith Wadson**, **Graeme Outerbridge**, **DeForest Trimingham**, and **Ian MacDonald-Smith**. **Will Collieson** works in a variety of media, often creating humorous collages.

Kathleen Helmsley-Bell creates exquisite dolls that represent actual people from Bermuda history. **Ronnie Chameaux's** carefully hand-crafted Christmas tree and table ornaments are little dolls made of the dried leaves of banana, grapefruit, and palm. The husband-and-wife team of **Jack** and **Celia Arnell** make intricately detailed miniature cedar furniture.

Calendar of Events

Run Bermuda

January/February

From January through March, the **Temperature Guarantee Programme** affords special visitor bonuses any time the temperature fails to reach 68°F (20°C). The day after the temperature fails to hit that mark, participating hotels offer a discount, admission is free to many sightseeing attractions, and price cuts are available on buses and ferries. The **Bermuda International Race Weekend** is an annual charity event that features marathon, half-marathon, and 10K races, and a 10K Charity Walk.

February is **Golden Rendezvous Month**, dedicated to visitors over 50, with events that include bus tours, lectures, bridge tournaments, ballroom dancing, and golf tournaments. The **Bermuda Festival** brings to the island renowned artists for classical music, dance, jazz, drama, and popular entertainment. Recent events include the Royal Winnipeg Ballet, the Empire Brass Quintet, and the National Black Touring Company. The **Lobster Pot Invitational** is an annual pro-amateur golf tournament, played at one of the island's spectacular golf clubs.

March/April

March through November is **racing season** in Bermuda, with many sailing and yachting events on these waters.

Spring Break, inspired by the US college holiday of the same name, lasts the whole of March, with events that include sports activities, a beach party, a boat cruise, artists' workshops, and other entertainments. The **Palm Sunday Walk** is an annual guided walking tour, sponsored by the Bermuda National Trust. The **Bermuda Kite Festival**, with competitions on Horseshoe Bay, games and lots of other events is held on Good Friday. The **Fun Run/Walk Around Harrington Sound**, is an annual fund-raiser in aid of the Bermuda Aquarium, Zoo and Natural History Museum.

The **Peppercorn Ceremony** takes places on the morning of the first Wednesday closest to 23 April, at which time the Masonic Lodge St George's No. 200 of the Grand Lodge of Scotland presents to the Mayor of the Town of St George its annual rent for the State House – one peppercorn, placed on a velvet pillow. April's **International Race Week** is a spectacular event on the Great Sound, with participating vessels including Sunfish, Comets, Snipes, Lasers, J-24s, IODs, and E-22s.

May/June

May is **Heritage Month**, when cultural and sporting events commemorate Bermuda's heritage. During the **Bermuda International Film Festival** in May, local theatres show high-quality independent films. The last Monday in May is **Bermuda Day** celebrated with a parade, marathon race, and other festivities. Also in May, the **Gombey Competition** is a thrilling spectacle, when Bermuda's famous Gombey Dancers, dressed in colourful traditional costume, compete for top honours.

In June, Newport, Rhode Island, and Annapolis, Maryland, are the US starting points and Bermuda the finishing line for yachts in the **Newport–Bermuda Race** and the **Bermuda Ocean Race**. Numerous events on and off the water contribute to the festive atmosphere. The third Monday in June is the official **Queen's Birthday**, which features parades, pomp, and ceremony.

July/August
In July's **Cup Match Cricket Festival**, the Somerset Cricket Club and the St George's Cricket Club compete in a two-day match. The **Non-Mariner's Race** is a hilarious event on the water, when homemade vessels race. The annual **Bank of Bermuda Triathlon Week** pits individuals and teams over two weekends.

Gearing up for cricket

September/October
The first Monday in September is **Labour Day**, a public holiday marked by a parade in Hamilton.

For October's **King Edward VII Gold Cup Match Racing**, an international roster of top-ranked Match Racing skippers compete on the water.

November/December
From **November until mid-March**, the Department of Tourism sponsors a host of events, most of them free. Among them are fashion shows, teas, and ballroom dancing, and a whole slew of sports activities such as golf, chess, and bridge tournaments.

The **Convening of Parliament** is the first Friday in November, when the Governor, garbed in full regalia, arrives in an open carriage at the Cabinet Building on Front Street.

In November, the **World Rugby Classic** features players from Bermuda, the US, Great Britain, Australia, France, and New Zealand for games played at the National Sports Club in Devonshire Parish.

Remembrance Day on 11 November, is marked by a parade on Front Street in Hamilton of veterans organisations, police, and the Bermuda Regiment.

During December, **Santa Claus parades** roll through Front Street, Hamilton, and King's Square, St George's.

The **St George's New Year's Eve Celebration** in King's Square features entertainment and a midnight countdown, with the lowering of the 'onion' followed by a fireworks display.

Food and Drink

It is doubtful that anyone makes a special pilgrimage to Bermuda to worship at the island's culinary shrines. But that is not to say there are no good restaurants. Indeed, there are some excellent eating establishments. Not surprisingly in this seafaring spot, sea creatures in various guises tend to dominate menus, and – again not surprisingly for this very British colony – pub fare is featured in cosy restaurants that would be right at home in rural England. But there are also restaurants that feature very good Asian, Mexican, Italian, French, and Continental cuisines. Pizza-lovers can find their favourite dish, and there are even a couple of KFCs in Hamilton, perhaps sneaked in while nobody was looking. There are no Burger Kings or McDonald's or other fast-food chains of that ilk. At least, not yet.

A Bermudian's traditional Sunday brunch is codfish cakes, served with boiled Irish potatoes, egg, and slices of banana and avocado. Fish chowder, spiked with dark rum and locally-made sherry peppers, is another local treat, as are the delicious spiny lobsters, available from September through March. And at Christmas, the special traditional dish is cassava pie. (Cassava is a root vegetable somewhat akin to the sweet potato).

Dining out is not cheap in Bermuda, since almost everything has to be imported. Don't be surprised if dinner for two at an upmarket restaurant runs upwards of $200. Most places accept credit cards, but some of the cottage colonies steadfastly refuse to take them. Remember, too, that a 15 percent service charge will be added to your bill. All of the cottage colonies, and many of the hotels, offer a range of meal plans, and your choice will make a substantial financial difference.

Chic dining

Dress during high season tends to be formal, though not necessarily – or even usually – tuxedos and long gowns. During low season dress may be casual, but it is never funky. 'Smart casual attire' is the term you'll hear all over the island, but high-end restaurants usually require a jacket and tie. In low season, some hotels and cottage colonies feature a 'casual night', but that only means ties are not required. Jackets for men are *de rigueur* the year-round.

Restaurant selection

Listings are in three categories: $$$$–$$$ = expensive; $$ = moderate; $ = inexpensive.

Bermudian
Green Lantern, 9 Serpentine Road, Hamilton, tel: 295-6995. Fish chowder, lobster in season, beef pies, fish and chips; very Bermudian, very un-touristy. $

Traditions, 2 Middle Road, Sandys Parish, tel: 234-3770. This is a charmer, in a little cottage near Port Royal Golf Club. **$**

Dennis's Hideaway, Cashew City Road, St David's Island, tel: 297-0044. Dennis Lamb, a true island character, serves up the likes of shark stew. Pick up a bottle of wine en route. **$$**

Paw Paw's, 87 South Road, Warwick Parish, tel: 236-7459. A blend of Bermudian, West Indian, and Continental cuisines; this is a good place to try the local Sunday brunch of codfish cakes and potatoes. **$$**

Plantation, Harrington Sound Road, Bailey's Bay, Hamilton Parish, tel: 293-1188. A plant-filled atrium setting at Leamington Caves. If you spend $10 or more, you get free entry to the caves. **$$**

Chinese

New Queen Restaurant, Par-la-Ville Road, Hamilton, tel: 295-4004. A tried and tested restaurant, featuring Szechuan cuisine. **$$**

Chopsticks, 88 Reid St, Hamilton, tel: 292-0791. Cantonese and Hunan, as well as Szechuan and a touch of Thai fare is served. **$$**

Continental

M. R. Onions, Par-la-Ville Road, Hamilton, tel: 292-5012. The name comes from the phrase 'Him are Onions'. Bermudians are called Onions because of the famed onion, grown here and exported in days gone by. This restaurant, a local favourite, serves onion soup, barbecue ribs, fish and chips; an early-bird special and children's menu are features. **$**

Carriage House, Water Street, St George's, tel: 297-1270 or 297-1730. Early bird specials, children's menu, and a good Sunday brunch, as well as moderately priced lunch, afternoon tea, and dinner. **$$**

Harbourfront, West Front Street, Hamilton, tel: 295-4207 or 295-6497. A local favourite, serving everything from sushi to seafood to entrecote. **$$**

Downtown dining at Ascots

Ascots, Royal Palm Hotel, 24 Rosemont Avenue, Hamilton, tel: 295-9644. On the outskirts of downtown Hamilton, an enormously popular place with dishes such as duck pâté and rack of lamb. **$$$**

Caliban's, South Road, Hamilton, tel: 236-1010. The fine dining room of Ariel Sands cottage colony (owned by actor Michael Douglas) serves lobster Thermidor, roast rack of lamb, and seafood, veal, and beef dishes. **$$$**

Margaret Rose, St George's Club, 6 Rose Hill, St George's, tel: 297-1301. The fine dining room of the St George's Club, offers guests breathtaking views of the water below. **$$$**

Caliban's

Norwood Room, Stonington Beach Hotel, Paget Parish, tel: 236-5416. Staffed by students training at the Hospitality and Culinary Institute; good service, lovely dining room. $$$

Authentic Bermudian cuisine

Cambridge Beaches, 30 Kings Point Road, Sandys Parish, tel: 234-0331. The main dining room of this elegant cottage colony has an intimate ambience and a menu that changes daily. $$$$

Fourways Inn, Middle Road, Paget, tel: 236-6517. An intimate 17th-century inn with selections such as Bermuda lobster, Chateaubriand, and Scottish smoked salmon. $$$$

Newport Room, Southampton Princess, tel: 238-8167. A chic dining room serving the likes of foie gras and caviar and vintage wines. $$$$

Romanoff, Church Street, Hamilton, tel: 295-0333. A handsome, formal restaurant for borscht, beef Stroganoff, chicken Kiev. Good wine list. $$$$

Tiara Room, Hamilton Princess Hotel, tel: 295-3000. A sweeping harbour view, elegant tableside service, and cherries jubilee, too. $$$$

Tom Moore's Tavern, Walsingham Lane, Hamilton Parish, tel: 293-8020. A 17th-century home, named for the Irish poet who lived briefly in Bermuda (but not in this house), with cuisine such as escargot, lobster, and roast duckling; a most impressive wine list. $$$$

French

Horizons, Middle Road, Paget Parish, tel: 236-6517. An intimate dining room, with a menu that changes daily; always fresh ingredients, good wine list. $$$$

Fresh food at Horizons

Waterlot Inn, Middle Road, Southampton Parish, tel: 238-0510. Candlelight dining in a 325-year-old waterside inn, one of the Southampton Princess Hotel's several eateries. $$$$

Indian
Bombay Bicycle Club, 75 Reid Street, Hamilton, tel: 292-0048 or 292-8865. Traditional Indian fare from a clay oven. $$

Italian
Speciality Inn, 4 South Road, Smith's Parish, tel: 236-3133. An inexpensive place in the small Collectors Hill shopping strip, very popular with locals. $

La Trattoria, 22 Washington Lane, Hamilton, tel: 295-1877. Casual and moderately priced Italian dining in a lane that connects Reid and Church Streets. $$

Pasta Basta, 1 Elliott St, Hamilton, tel: 295-9785. A casual Northern Italian place for homemade pastas. **Pasta Pasta** in York Street, St George's is a sibling. $$

Portofino, Bermudiana Road, Hamilton, tel: 292-2375 or 295-6090. Dinner only, featuring fettuccini Alfredo, lasagna and veal parmegiana. $$

Ristorante Primavera, West Front Street, Hamilton, tel: 295-2167. Northern Italian food; lunch and dinner. $$

Tio Pepe, South Road, Southampton Parish, tel: 238-1897 or 238-0572. A casual Italian restaurant (pizzas are featured) masquerading under a Mexican name. Dining indoors or out. $$

Il Palio, 64 Middle Road, Sandys Parish, tel: 234-1049. A small informal place for Northern Italian cuisine, open for dinner only. $$$

Little Venice, Bermudiana Road, Hamilton, tel: 295-3503. Northern Italian fare; dinner includes admission to The Club for dancing. $$$

Japanese
The Mikado, Marriott's Castle Harbour Hotel, tel: 293-2040. Sake, sushi, and Teppanyaki, too. $$$

Mexican
Rosa's Cantina, 121 Front St, Hamilton, tel: 295-2912. Tex-Mex fare in a pleasant spot with Mexican decor and good Mexican beer. $$

Pubs
Freddie's Pub on the Square, King's Square, St George's, tel: 297-1717. A marvellous location, smack on King's Square, complete with balcony dining. $$

Frog & Onion Pub, The Cooperage, Royal Naval Dockyard, tel: 234-2900. Dining indoors or al fresco; pub fare, seafood, and steaks. $$

Henry VIII, South Road, Southampton Parish, tel: 238-1977. Very Merrie Olde England theme restaurant with raucous live entertainment, draws mostly tourists. $$$

Good choice at the Frog & Onion

Hog Penny, 5 Burnaby Street, Hamilton, tel: 292-2534. Bangers and mash, steak and kidney pie, and shepherd's pie are the Hog Penny's specialities. **$$**

Somerset Country Squire, Somerset Village, tel: 234-0105. A cosy pub just off beautiful Mangrove Bay, not far from Cambridge Beaches. **$$**

Swizzle Inn, Blue Hole Hill, Bailey's Bay, 293-1854. Very popular pub with lots of atmosphere, near the Bermuda Perfumery and Bermuda Glassblowing Studio. **$$**

Try a Rum Swizzle

Seafood

Freeport Seafood Restaurant, 1 Freeport Road, Royal Naval Dockyard, tel: 234-1692. Dining inside or outside, just past the entrance to Dockyard. Casual. **$**

Fisherman's Reef, 5 Burnaby Street, Hamilton, tel: 292-1609. A casual place with a live lobster tank, and surf and turf dishes. **$$**

Lobster Pot, 6 Bermudiana Road, Hamilton, tel: 292-6898. A long-time favourite place. **$$**

Port of Call, 87 Front Street, Hamilton, tel: 295-5373. Snappy nautical decor and fresh seafood. **$$**

Whaler Inn, Southampton Princess, Southampton Parish, tel: 238-0076. A dramatic setting and seafare for lunch and dinner. **$$$**

Catch of the day

Light fare

Ice Queen, Queen Street, Hamilton, tel: 292-6497; Rural Hill, Paget, tel: 236-3136. Casual burger places, open till late **$**.

Lighthouse Tearoom, Gibbs Hill Lighthouse, Southampton Parish, tel: 238-8679. At the base of Gibb's Hill Lighthouse, serving breakfast, lunch (salads and sandwiches), and afternoon tea, with crumpets and scones. **$**

Mrs Tea's Victorian Tea Room, 25 Middle Road, Southampton Parish, tel: 234-1374. A charming tea room for lunch and traditional English tea, with fresh scones, clotted cream, and jam. **$**

Take Five, Washington Mall (upstairs), Hamilton, tel: 295-4903. A cafe popular with visitors and locals, serving a traditional Bermudian breakfast on Saturday. **$**

The Spot, Burnaby Street, Hamilton, tel: 292-6293. A coffee shop serving plain fare in downtown Hamilton, always flooded with office workers at lunchtime. **$**

Steaks

The Colony Pub, Hamilton Princess Hotel, Pitts Bay Road, Hamilton, tel: 295-3000. A New York-style steak house, very popular with locals as well as visitors. **$$$**

The Rib Room, Southampton Princess Hotel, Southampton Parish, tel: 238-8223. The house speciality is hickory-smoked prime rib. **$$$**

Regimental welcome

Nightlife

Bars and discos

During the summer high season, all of the resort hotels and cottage colonies have some form of live entertainment – often calypso music, but other forms as well – most evenings. Even in low season, a standard hotel feature is the Monday night rum swizzle party,where guests mingle and enjoy a rum.

Disco is still alive in Bermuda, in Hamilton at the **Club** (Bermudiana Rd, tel: 295-9627) and the **Oasis** (Emporium Bldg., Front St, tel: 292-4978). Other popular nightclubs in Hamilton are the **Odyssey** (Front St, tel: 296-4390), the **Spinning Wheel** (Court St, tel: 292-7799), and **Pier 6** (Front St, tel: 292-6566). **Hubie's Bar** (Angle St, tel: 293-9287) features jazz on Friday nights, and **Casey's Bar** (Queen St, tel: 293-9549) is a popular after-work hangout. Still in Hamilton, **Robin Hood** (Richmond Rd, tel: 295-3314), and the **Cock & Feather** (Front St, tel: 295-2263), are other highly favoured bars. At Dockyard, **Club 21** (tel: 234-2721), open only in high season, is an intimate jazz club, and folks in St George's flock to the **Wharf Tavern** (Water St, tel: 297-1515) to knock back a few. The **Clayhouse Inn** (North Shore Rd., tel: 292-3193), a waterside club, does rousing calypso and limbo shows.

The mood is relaxed

Cinema

Bermuda has four first-run cinemas. Two are in Hamilton: the Liberty Theatre on Court Street, and the Little Theatre on Queen Street. The Neptune is at the Royal Naval Dockyard, in the Cooperage across from the Maritime Museum. The New Somers Theatre is on Duke of York Street in St George's. Bermuda's daily newspaper, the *Royal Gazette*, has a listing for them.

Shopping

Shopping is a major tourist pursuit on the island. Bermudian merchants buy cashmere, woollens, tweeds and other goods direct from the manufacturers, which means hefty discounts, and substantial savings. Top-quality cameras, watches, electronics, linens, perfumes, crystal and china are also sold below US prices. In some cases, as in the Louis Vuitton boutique, prices may be the same as in the United States, but there is no sales tax in Bermuda, so the price on the tag is what you pay.

The primary shopping centre for Bermuda is the capital city of Hamilton, where **Front Street** is lined with small arcaded buildings painted in pastel colours and trimmed in white. Several alleyways thread from Front to Reid Street and from Reid to Church Street. There are clusters of shops, eateries, and art galleries in the **Bermudiana Mall**, and in the **Emporium** and **Butterfield Place**, both on Front Street. **Windsor Place** is a mall on Queen Street, and the **Washington Mall** sits between Reid and Church streets, accessible via Washington Lane which cuts through from Reid to Church. **Chancery Lane** and **The Walkway**, both dotted with shops, are passageways that thread through from Front to Reid streets.

Everything Bermudian

In the east end, St George's is the Bermuda beacon for shoppers, in particular **Water Street**, off King's Square, and restored wharves, **Somers**, **Hunter's**, and **Penno's**. The **Clocktower Centre** at Royal Naval Dockyard in the west end is chock-a-block with boutiques and art galleries.

Bermuda's long-established department stores are **Trimingham's** (tel: 295-1183), **H.A. & E. Smith's** (tel: 295-2288), and **A.S. Cooper & Sons** (tel: 295-3961). The main stores for each are on Front Street in Hamilton; there are also branches in St George's, Dockyard, and in large resort hotels in the parishes. There is also a Front Street branch of the British chainstore **Marks & Spencer** ('Marks & Sparks' as it's often called – tel: 295-0031). Other well-known shops for clothing are **Archie Brown** (tel: 295-2928) and the **English Sports Shop** (tel: 295-2672). Women's high fashions can also be found at **Triangle's** (tel: 292-1990), **Cecile** (tel: 295-1311), and **Calypso** (tel: 295-2112) in Hamilton. Italian designer **Stephanel** (tel: 295-5698) is represented in his shop on Reid Street, Hamilton.

Jill Amos Raines

For made-in-Bermuda souvenirs try the unique crafts at the **Bermuda Arts Centre** and the **Crafts Market** at Dockyard. In Bailey's Bay the handmade glass collectibles made in the **Bermuda Glassblowing Studio** are at once practical and works of art. The essences made from island blossoms such as Frangipani, Passion Flower and Jasmine are a speciality of the **Bermuda Perfumery**.

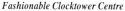

Fashionable Clocktower Centre

Jobson's Cove

Active Pursuits

Beaches

Bermuda's beaches really are pink. That isn't just public relations puff stuff. The soft pink colour is a result of infinitesimal bits of shell and coral that wash ashore from the reefs. The best beaches by far are on the south shore; the northern coast is for the most part rocky and barren, apart from sandy Shelly Bay, although people do swim off the rocky coast. The showcase beach on the south shore is **Horseshoe Bay** but it's actually one of a long stretch of heavenly beaches that extend all the way from Tucker's Town into Southampton Parish, and include **Warwick Long Bay**, **Chaplin Bay**, and **Jobson's Cove**. **Elbow Beach** also brings on an attack of hyperbole, and there's only a small fee for using the Elbow Beach Hotel's beach facilities. **Tobacco Bay** and **St Catherine's** Beach on St George's Island are lovely, and at Tobacco Bay there's a snack bar and facilities for changing and renting snorkelling equipment. Bermuda's public beaches are for the most part untended; there are lifeguards at only a few, and then only during high season and, in some cases, only on weekends. Since beach changing facilities are also scarce, what you do is wear your swimsuit under your clothes. Do not wear a swimsuit on the street without a covering: Bermudians frown on immodest attire.

Golf

Bermuda is renowned for its golf courses. There are eight of them on the island – more golf links per square mile than any place else on the planet. Because of the mild climate, golfing can be enjoyed all year, but strong cantankerous winds are also a factor the year-round.

Year-round golf

Bermuda's dress code extends to golfers; proper attire is required. Shirts must have collars and sleeves, and shorts must be Bermuda length. No jeans, gyms shorts, or cut-offs are allowed. An introduction by a member is required at the private **Mid-Ocean Club** and at the **Riddell's Bay Golf Club**. Bermuda Government courses (Port Royal, Ocean View, and St George's Golf Club) have a centralised, automated Tee Time Reservation System (295-6500). For private courses it is necessary to arrange in advance starting times through hotel and guest house managements.

Tennis

The island is virtually carpeted with tennis courts. There are three Government-run courts open to the general public: the **Government Tennis Stadium** (2 Marsh Folly Rd, Hamilton, tel: 292-0105) the **Port Royal Club** (Middle Rd, Southampton, tel: 234-0974) in the west end, and the **Kindley Community Tennis Courts** (Water St, tel: 297-1754) in St George's. As with golf, proper attire is required on the tennis courts.

Watersports

Yachting, sailing, and watersports of all kinds are, quite naturally, very actively pursued. All hotels can arrange watersports, and the larger properties have on-site facilities. Glass-bottom and other sightseeing boats take on passengers in Hamilton Harbour, next to the Ferry Terminal building on Front Street. Needless to say, snorkelling and scuba diving are splendid. There are more than 300 wrecked vessels in Bermuda's beautiful but hazardous reefs.

Snorkelling and diving can be arranged through **South Side Scuba** (293-2915); **Fantasea Diving** (236-6339); **Blue Water Divers** (234-1034); and **Nautilus Diving** (238-2322).

Fishing

Fishermen will find themselves in hog heaven, as it were, as Bermuda is considered one of the world's finest fishing centres, especially when it comes to light tackle fishing. Offshore fishers go for Wahoo, Amberjack, Rainbow Runner, Great Barracuda, Blue Marlin, Blackfin Tuna, and Yellowfin Tuna. Reef fishers seek school-size Greater Amberjack and Aimaco Jack, Great Barracuda, Little Tunny, Bermuda Chub, Gray Snapper, Yellowfin Snapper, and assorted bottom fish.

Spear fishing is strictly prohibited within one mile of Bermuda's shores. An aqualung may not be used to spear fish, and a spear gun may not be used at any time.

As with other water-related sports, all hotels can arrange fishing expeditions.

85

Watersports of all kinds
Parasailing view

Getting There

By air

The only regularly-scheduled year-round way to arrive in Bermuda is by air. The great majority of visitors to Bermuda come from Canada, England, and the US, especially the US east coast.

From the US, **American Airlines** (800-433-7300) has daily non-stop service from New York's JFK Airport, and seasonal non-stop service from Boston Logan International Airport (March to October). **Continental** (800-231-0856) flies daily non-stop from Newark Airport; **Delta Air Lines** (800-221-1212) has daily non-stop service from Boston and Atlanta; and **US Airways** (800-428-4322) flies daily non-stop from Baltimore/Washington, Charlotte, NC, Philadelphia, and New York (LaGuardia). **Air Canada** (800-776-3000), whose US partners are Continental and United Airlines (800-241-6522), has non-stop service from Toronto and Halifax, with connecting flights throughout Canada, the US and Europe. **British Airways** (800-247-9297 in the US, 0181-897-4000 in London, 0345-222-111 outside London) has daily non-stop service from London's Gatwick Airport.

An aerial view of the airport

In addition, there are some charter flights landing here, but because of the island's small size and limited facilities, they are carefully regulated by the Bermuda Government, especially during peak season (mid-April until the end of October).

Bermuda's modern terminal, **Kindley Field**, is located in the east end on St George's Island. The airport is about 14 km (9 miles) from Hamilton, the capital city, and about 27 km (17 miles) from the west end of the island. Bermuda is so tiny that everyone remotely involved in tourism knows exactly what time planes arrive, so there are always taxis at the airport awaiting each arrival. Some hotels have limousine service to and from Kindley Field. The airport is also on the public bus route, but if you have a lot of luggage this can be a rather arduous way to reach your destination.

By ship

The Bermuda Government also regulates the number and size of cruise ships that may call during peak season. Several cruise lines operate from various ports the year round, including Cunard's grand *Queen Elizabeth 2*, but during peak season there is regularly scheduled weekly service from New York by **Royal Caribbean Cruise Lines'** *Song of America*; **Celebrity Cruise Lines'** *Horizon* and *Zenith*; and **Norwegian Cruise Lines'** *Norwegian Crown*.

The only other option for arriving on water is via private yacht, and this seafaring island-nation has a sizeable yachting community.

Cruise in to Hamilton Harbour

Catch the ferry from the harbour

Getting Around

By bus

The pink-and-blue buses of the Public Transportation Board (292-3854) cover the island, operating from the central terminal on Washington Street in Hamilton, near City Hall, and stopping at many tourist attractions and beaches. Exact fare is required. Those planning to make frequent use of the buses should stop by the terminal to buy a Multi-Day Pass. Available for one, three, or seven days, the passes provide for unlimited bus and ferry transport. The 'Bus & Ferry Schedules' brochure, with a map, routes, and schedules, is available at the bus and ferry terminals, at visitors' service centres, and at most hotels and guest houses. In addition, the West End Mini-Bus (234-2344) operates between Somerset Bridge and Royal Naval Dockyard; the East End Mini-Bus (297-8492) scoots around St George's and St David's Islands; and Suburban Transit Mini-Bus (235-5299 or 234-8986) runs between Pembroke and Devonshire parishes. The buses run daily, but hours are sometimes limited during the winter, low season when it is less busy.

By ferry

Ferries depart from the Marine and Ports Terminal on Front Street in Hamilton (295-4506), crossing Hamilton Harbour to Paget and Warwick parishes and the Great Sound to Somerset parish and the Royal Naval Dockyard. The Paget and Warwick routes take five to ten minutes; Hamilton to Dockyard is more than an hour. Mopeds and bikes can be taken (at extra charge) on the Somerset ferry, but not on the smaller Harbour ferries. The Paget ferry stops at Lower Ferry, Hodson's Landing, and Salt Kettle, while the Warwick ferry pulls in at Darrell's Wharf and Belmont

Landing. The Somerset ferry is a bit tricky, and you must study the timetable carefully. Some ferries go from Hamilton directly to Dockyard, a trip of an hour and 15 minutes, while others stop first at Somerset Bridge, a mere 20 minutes from Hamilton, before going on to Dockyard. Monday to Saturday, Paget and Warwick ferries operate until 11.30pm. Be aware that the last ferry from Hamilton to Somerset leaves at 5.20pm, and that on Sunday the ferry service ends with the last trip to Hamilton at 7.37pm.

By taxi

The Bermuda Government regulates and licenses the island's taxis, all of which have meters and two-way radios. Most of the cars are spotless, and the drivers friendly. Many are licensed tour guides, and will give running commentary on points of interest. Available at the airport, at major hotels, and in response to telephone calls, the air-conditioned 4-passenger or 6-passenger taxis can also be hailed on the streets, and can be rented by the hour, by the day, or by the meter – a good alternative for sightseers who do not want to go the moped route. Taxi services include **Radio Cabs** (295-4141) and **Bermuda Taxi Operators** (292-5600). Wheelchair accessible service is provided by **Wheelchair Taxi Service** (236-1456); advance notice is advised.

By moped or motor scooter

There are no car rentals on the island. Because of Bermuda's size, only property owners may own a car, and only one car per household is allowed. The most pervasive mode of tourist transportation is the moped, or motor scooter. (Motor scooters are larger and more powerful than mopeds.) Single-seat or double-seat mopeds and scooters can be rented by the hour, the day, or the week. There are cycle liveries at several locations around the island, some of which have branches at hotels. But cycles are not without risk. Remember to drive on the *left*. There are numerous accidents involving tourists unaccustomed to cycles, and/or driving on the left. Night riding or riding on rain-slick roads can be particularly hazardous. (Bermudians are not excessively tolerant of tourists on mopeds.) Be on the look-out for 'sleeping policemen' (speed bumps), especially on approaches to cottage colonies and hotels; otherwise, they can come as a rude awakening. The strictly enforced speed limit is 35 kph (20 mph). Rentals include helmets (mandatory), lock and key, basket, and compulsory third-party insurance; a deposit is required. Drivers must be at least 16 years of age. Among the reliable cycle liveries offering free pickup and delivery are **Eve Cycles** (236-6247); **Oleander Cycles** (295-0919); and **Wheels Cycles** (295-0112).

Drive on the left

Facts for the Visitor

Passports and visas

Passports are required for entry, as well as a return or on-ward ticket. Passengers arriving with an open return ticket will have a time limit imposed. Applications to extend the length of stay must be made in person at the Immigration Headquarters in Hamilton. Passengers arriving without a return ticket or on a one-way ticket into Bermuda will not be admitted unless prior Bermuda Immigration authorisation has been given.

Customs

In addition to personal items, visitors may bring in duty free 1 litre (one quart) of wine; 1 litre (one quart) spirits; 200 cigarettes; ½ kg (one pound) of tobacco; 50 cigars; and $30 worth of gifts. On departure, US citizens go through American Customs at the Bermuda Airport.

Departure taxes

The $20 airport departure tax and $60 departure tax for cruise ship passengers are included in your fare.

Tourist information

The **Bermuda Department of Tourism** (43 Church St, Hamilton HM 12, Bermuda) publishes tons of brochures about the island, including *Where to Stay*, *What to Do*, and *Shopping*. The brochures are available by writing to the main office, and also at the visitors centres, located in the ferry terminal in Hamilton, on King's Square in St George's, and in the Clocktower Centre at Royal Naval Dockyard. Other complimentary visitors guides include *Key to Attractions*, *Key to the City*, *Preview of Bermuda*, and *This Week in Bermuda*, which are also available in the visitors centres and most hotels and guest houses.

Finding your way around is easy

Media

Bermuda's morning newspaper, the *Royal Gazette*, published daily except Sunday, carries local and international news as well as calendars of events, etc. The *Bermuda Sun* and the *Mid-Ocean News* are weekly newspapers. *The Bermudian*, a slick monthly magazine, and *Bermuda Magazine*, a glossy quarterly, are sold at newsstands. *Vacation Bermuda*, placed in most guest rooms, is a hard cover publication with information about restaurants, nightlife, sightseeing, and so forth, but because it is printed annually it is not as current as other publications.

Most hotels and guest houses subscribe to the Bermuda cable system, which offers more than 50 channels including the BBC and US sports and entertainment channels. 'The Bermuda Channel' airs tourism-related programmes.

Currency and exchange

The Bermuda Dollar ($BD), which is divided into 100 cents, is pegged to the US dollar, which means that US currency is accepted anywhere on the island at face value. US travellers cheques are also accepted island-wide. Other foreign currencies are not accepted, but may be exchanged in local banks at rates that are set daily. Banking hours vary slightly from bank to bank, but are roughly from 9am until 3pm or 4pm Monday through Friday.

A fistful of dollars

Dress

Bermuda is much more formal than islands with a similar climate in the Caribbean. Casual resort wear – slacks and walking shorts – is acceptable during the day, but bathing suits, halters, and short-shorts are not worn on the streets, or, indeed, anywhere except on the beach. It is virtually unheard of, and in fact highly objectionable for a man to appear on the streets without a shirt. Cover-ups for swimmers should be worn even in hotel lobbies. Bermudians dress for dinner, and while that does not mean formalwear it does mean, in the local vernacular, 'smart casual' attire. When Bermudian men 'dress up', they wear a tie and jacket with the famed Bermuda shorts and proper knee-length socks. During the summer it is wise to bring cotton clothing; it doesn't pack as well as synthetics, but it's cooler. During the winter (or 'spring') months, lightweight woollens will do the trick.

91

Electricity

Bermuda electrical current is the same as the US and Canada: 110 volt, 60 AC. Visitors from the UK and other European countries will need an adaptor.

Tipping

In lieu of tipping, hotels and guest houses add 10 percent (or a fixed amount) per person per day to the bill. The service charge covers bell and maid service and some dining room services, depending upon the type of meal plan chosen. (On MAP plans, charges range from $11 to $15.50 per diem.) Many restaurants include a 15 percent service charge in the tally. For those that do not, a tip of 15 percent is customary.

Daily mail collections

Postal services

The **General Post Office** is on Church Street in Hamilton. The historic Perot Post Office is on Queen Street, also in Hamilton. Postage rates to the US and Canada (up to 10 grams) is 65 cents for first-class airmail letters and 60 cents for first-class airmail postcards. Rates to the UK (up to 10 grams) is 80 cents for first-class airmail letters, and 75 cents for first-class airmail postcards.

Public holidays

On public holidays and Sundays, all shops, businesses, and many restaurants close down. Buses and ferries run on limited schedules. Most sightseeing attractions are open, and sports activities are available. Public holidays that coincide with a Sunday are normally observed the following day. Where public holidays coincide with a Saturday, Government and commercial offices are closed the following Monday or Tuesday, but restaurants and shops remain open. Public holidays are: New Year's Day (1 January), Good Friday, Bermuda Day (in May), Queen's Birthday (third Monday in June), Cup Match/Somers Day (the Thursday and Friday before the first Monday in August), Labour Day (first Monday in September), Remembrance Day (11 November), Christmas Day (25 December), and Boxing Day (26 December).

A very British telephone box

Telephone

The area code for Bermuda is **441**. To direct dial the US, dial 1+area code+number. For international calls, the International Direct Dial access code is 011, followed by the country code and the number. Most hotels levy a surcharge of 75 cents to one dollar on outside calls, even international calls charged to a credit card. The surcharge can be avoided by using the facilities of **Cable & Wireless** (20 Front Street, 24-hour help line, tel: 297-7022) or **Tele-Bermuda International** (8 Par-la-Ville Road, tel: 296-9000). Remember that faxes are usually cheaper than phone calls.

Time

Bermuda is in the Atlantic Time Zone. Bermuda Standard Time is Greenwich Mean Time (GMT) minus four hours, and one hour ahead of Eastern Standard Time (EST). Daylight Savings Time runs from the first Sunday in April until the last Sunday in October.

Keeping Bermuda time

Water

The drinking water is perfectly safe. However, there are no freshwater lakes on the island and it must depend upon rainfall to replenish the supply. During dry spells, hotels usually post little signs requesting guests to kindly conserve water.

Medical Assistance

Bermuda's hospital is **King Edward VII Memorial Hospital** (7 Point Finger Road, Paget, tel: 236-2345), a modern facility with an emergency room open 24 hours. Physician and dentist referrals are available at the **Government Health Clinic** (67 Victoria Street, Hamilton, tel: 236-0224). For emergency police, fire, and ambulance, call **911**.

Accommodation

A good place to relax

For so tiny an island, Bermuda offers an astonishing array of accommodation, from cosy guest houses and self-catering apartments to splashy resorts and elegant cottage colonies. The latter are oceanfront properties of considerable acreage, with dining room, bar, etc in a main building, and guest rooms and suites in individual cottages. In the larger properties there is usually a byzantine choice of meal plans, and your selection can greatly alter your bottom line. American Plan (AP) means all meals are included; Modified American Plan (MAP) includes breakfast and dinner; Bermuda Plan (BP) is a full, hearty breakfast; Continental Plan (CP) is Continental breakfast only; and European Plan (EP) has no meals included. Some of the cottage colonies offer only MAP. Selecting AP or MAP means having all meals at your hotel. But it's wise to remember that dining out is pricey.

The Bermuda Department of Tourism licenses all categories of accommodation, inspecting each and imposing rigid standards. Properties listed in the tourist department's brochures are top-quality, but not necessarily elegant.

Hotels are sprinkled all around the island, though the greatest concentration is along the south shore, which has the island's finest beaches. Nothing in Bermuda can actually be called 'cheap', but there are some less expensive guest houses along South Road that are within walking distance of surf and sand. If you're willing to eschew a slew of restaurants and bars in a hotel and don't mind walking across the road to a public beach, you can save money by booking one of these guest houses.

Hamilton is home to the island's dowager Princess Hotel, as well as to several guest houses. If shopping is important, you may prefer staying in 'the city.' Some of Hamilton's guest houses, as well as other beachless prop-

The Princess Hotel

erties around the island, have arrangements whereby their guests may use the facilities at the Coral Beach Club or the Mid-Ocean Club, two posh private clubs on the south shore.

There are fewer options in the far eastern and western parts of island, but distances are not great – only 34 km (21 miles) separate the East End from the West End. And Sandys Parish, in the West End, is home to Bermuda's most elegant cottage colony, Cambridge Beaches.

The rates indicated apply during the summer high season. During low season – from about late November until late March – prices are substantially lower.

Following are some suggestions in several categories: $$$$=Very Expensive; $$$=Expensive; $$=Moderate; $=Inexpensive.

Cottage Colonies

Cambridge Beaches, 30 King's Point, Sandys MA 02, tel: 234-0331; fax: 234-3352. Sits on a private West End peninsula edged with pink beaches. **$$$$**; **Fourways Inn**, in Paget Parish, tel: 236-5528. A stately place with a formal ambience and superb restaurant, not far from south shore beaches. **$$$$**; **Horizons & Cottages**, 33 South Road, tel: 236-0048. A Relais & Chateau property, guests enjoy the facilities of a private beach club on the south shore, also has a fine restaurant. **$$$$**; **Pink Beach Club** is on the south shore, in Tuckers Town, near Harrington Sound. **$$$$**; **Ariel Sands**, PO Box HM 334, Hamilton HM BX, tel: 236-1010; fax: 236-0087. On the south shore, with a spectacular beach and two ocean-fed pools. **$$$**; **Willowbank**, PO Box MA 296, Sandys MA BX, tel: 234-1616; fax: 234-3373. A quiet alternative retreat from the flashy resort hotels, is near beautiful Ely's Harbour. **$$**.

Resort Hotels

Southampton Princess, PO Box HM 1379 HM FX, tel: 238-8000; fax: 238-8968. A big splashy hotel, with a south shore beach and several restaurants and bars. **$$$$**; **Elbow Beach**, PO Box HM 455, Hamilton HM BX, tel: 236-3535; fax: 236-8043. Flashy place on one of the south shore's best beaches. **$$$$**; **Belmont Hotel & Golf Club**, PO Box WK 251, Warwick WK BX, tel: 236-1301; fax: 236-6867. No beach, but it is a favourite of golfers. **$$**; **Marriott's Castle Harbour**, PO Box HM 841, Hamilton CM CX, tel: 293-2040; fax: 293-8288. A big modern convention hotel on Castle Harbour. **$$$**; **Sonesta Beach Resort**, PO Box HM 1070, Hamilton HM EX, tel: 238-8122; fax: 238-8463. The only property on which you can walk directly from your room onto a sandy beach. **$$$**; **Hamilton Princess**, PO Box 837, Hamilton HM CX, tel: 295-3000; fax: 295-1914. This is a sedate grande dame

Horizons on the south shore

The pier at Willowbank

hotel whose guests use beach and other facilities of its sister the Southampton Princess. $$$.

Small Hotels

The Reefs, 56 South Road, Southampton SN 02, tel: 238-0222; fax: 238-8372. An elegant hotel on a smashing south shore beach. $$$$; **Waterloo House**, PO Box HM 333, Hamilton HM BX, tel: 295-4480; fax: 295-2585. A posh small hotel on Hamilton Harbour. $$$$; **Pompano Beach Club**, 36 Pompano Beach Road, Southampton SB 03, tel: 234-0222; fax: 234-1694. This is a casually elegant sport-oriented hotel. $$$; **Royal Palms**, PO Box HM 499, Hamilton HM CX, tel: 292-1834; fax: 292-1946. A former private home, with a popular restaurant, on a hilltop near Front Street's shops and restaurants. $$.

Guest Houses

Aunt Nea's Inn at Hillcrest, PO Box GE 96, St. George's GE BX, tel: 297-1630; fax: 297-1908. Tucked among St George's alleyways, is this charming bed-and-breakfast. $$; **Oxford House**, PO Box HM 374, Hamilton HM BX, tel: 295-0503; fax: 295-0250. Delightful rooms and Continental breakfast near Hamilton's Front Street. $$; **Edgehill Manor**, PO Box HM 1048, Hamilton HM EX, tel: 295-7124; fax: 295-3850. Friendly bed-and-breakfast. $; **Salt Kettle House**, 10 Salt Kettle Road, Paget PG 01, tel: 236-0407; fax: 236 8639. On the harbour across from Hamilton, is a wonderful guest house, offering hearty breakfasts. $; **Royal Heights**, PO Box SN 144, Southampton SN BX, tel: 238-0043; fax: 238-8445. A lovely bed-and-breakfast near Gibbs Hill Lighthouse and the south shore. Large rooms with spectacular views. $.

95

Self-Catering Apartments

Grape Bay Cottages, PO Box PG 137, Paget PG BX, tel: 236-1194; fax: 236-3290. A great honeymoon option, two private cottages a few steps from Grape Bay Beach. $$; **Marley Beach**, PO Box PG 78, Paget PG BX, tel: 236-1143; fax: 236-1984. Excellent for families or friends travelling together. Cottages overlooking a pretty beach. $$; **Astwood Cove**, 49 South Road, Warwick WK 07, tel: 236-0984; fax: 236-1164. Simple but spotless apartments just across the road from the public south shore beaches. $$; **Skytop Cottages**, PO Box PG 227, Paget PG BX, tel: 236-7984; fax: 232-0446. Lovely hilltop views, near south shore beaches. $$; **Angel's Grotto**, PO Box HS 81, Harrington Sound HS BX, tel: 293-1986; fax: 294-4164. A cluster of beautifully decorated cottages, a short distance from the beach at John Smith's Bay. $; **Brightside Apartments**, PO Box FL 319, Smith's FL BX, tel: 292-8410; fax: 295-6968. Simple but clean, near the Aquarium. $.

Marley Beach

Index